New York

CULT RECIPES

MARC GROSSMAN

New York

CULT RECIPES

photographs
AKIKO IDA AND PIERRE JAVELLE

illustrations of New York
JANE TEASDALE

styling
SABRINA FAUDA-RÔLE

art direction
FABIENNE CORON

MURDOCH BOOKS

THE CULT RECIPES OF A NEW YORKER

My grandparents emigrated to New York from Russia. I went in the opposite direction and consequently have spent the last 13 years as a New Yorker in Paris. People are always asking me if I miss New York and seem shocked that I chose to leave. The truth is I like being a New Yorker in Paris more than being a New Yorker in New York, where, let's face it, we're a dime a dozen. It's kind of like Superman. On earth, he's a superhero — *faster than a speeding bullet … able to leap tall buildings in a single bound*. But back on Krypton (with its presumably higher gravitational pull), he'd just be one Kryptonian among others, a mere pedestrian going about his not-particularly heroic business. Not to suggest that New Yorkers are some sort of super race or that living there is a bore, but being an expat does have its perks. For starters, you get to actually miss and appreciate all those things you once took for granted. And if you're like me, this phenomenon will manifest itself almost exclusively through food. What begins as a minor homesick craving — say, for a fresh bialy from Kossar's or a piece of cheesecake from Junior's — builds into a full-blown culinary obsession. The next thing you know you've spent two weeks trying to make the perfect fill-in-the-blank from your composite food memories, which pretty much explains this book. Basically, these are the recipes I crave most when I miss New York and, as such, they reflect my own idiosyncratic experience of New York food — a mix of Greek diners, Jewish delis, old-school Chinatown, American junk food, American health food and a bunch of other stuff tossed into the melting pot. Put it all together and you've got a one-way ticket to NYC. Enjoy the flight! **M.G.**

7 : 10
COFFEE TIME

FILTERED COFFEE

Unlimited refills of filtered coffee is a longstanding tradition in New York diners. We call it a bottomless cup, and this is surely one of the reasons why New York is called 'the city that never sleeps'. In recent years, the once-humble cup of filtered coffee has been gaining in prestige as a new wave of coffee afficionados work on preparing it with scientific precision using freshly ground coffee beans. My friend Thomas Lehoux, one of the founders of the Parisian coffee club Frog Fight and co-owner of Café Réné, was one of the first to promote this style of coffee in Paris. Here are his instructions for making a perfect cup at home.

MAKES 1 CUP

Preparation time: 5 minutes

WHAT YOU NEED

a kettle
a dripper (preferably Hario®)
a coffee pot
a filter (preferably Kalita®)
freshly roasted whole coffee beans
a set of scales
a coffee grinder

Step 1. Boil some water in the kettle.
Step 2. Put the dripper on the coffee pot and the filter into the dripper. When the water boils, pour a little into the filter to rinse it out and remove the paper taste. Warm the coffee pot as well.
Step 3. Weigh out the coffee. The general rule is: 60 g (2¼ oz) coffee to 1 litre (35 fl oz/4 cups) water. So for 400 ml (14 fl oz) water, I use 25 g (1 oz) coffee. Grind the coffee to filter coffee size — you should be able to feel the particles between your fingers. It looks like a powder to the eye.
Step 4. Put the coffee in the middle of the filter and add 80 ml (2½ fl oz/⅓ cup) water. Wait for 30 seconds (to de-gas the coffee), then slowly add the remaining 320 ml (11 fl oz) water. It should take about 2½ minutes for all the water to filter through to your coffee pot (if this is not the case, grind the coffee more finely and increase the volume of water). Don't stir the coffee grinds with a spoon, let the water flow through by itself.
Step 5. Enjoy your coffee.

ICED COFFEE

Use the same method, adding ice to the jug after rinsing the filter, and reduce the equivalent weight of the ice from the water.

CHALLAH

*This braided loaf, traditionally eaten for Shabbat,
is New York's answer to the French brioche.*

MAKES 1 LOAF

Preparation time: 45 minutes, plus cooling
Resting time: 2½ hours
Cooking time: 25 minutes

DRY INGREDIENTS

575 g (1 lb 4½ oz) plain (all-purpose) flour
1½ teaspoons dried yeast
55 g (2 oz/¼ cup) caster (superfine) sugar
2 teaspoons fine salt

WET INGREDIENTS

145 ml (4¾ fl oz) lukewarm water
2 eggs
2 egg yolks
2 tablespoons olive oil

GLAZE

1 tablespoon egg white
1 teaspoon caster (superfine) sugar

THE DOUGH

Combine the dry ingredients, then beat together the wet ingredients.
Carefully combine the two mixtures and knead until the dough is
very elastic (5–10 minutes in a machine, 10–20 minutes by hand).
Form a smooth ball of dough, place it in an oiled container
and cover with plastic wrap. Let it rise at room temperature
for about 1½ hours until it has doubled in volume.

SHAPING THE DOUGH

Divide the dough into six equal portions. Using the palms of
your hands, shape each portion into evenly shaped sausages
about 30 cm (12 inches) long. On a baking tray that's
floured or lined with baking paper, braid the sausages using
the illustration as a guide. Sprinkle the braid lightly with
flour, then cover loosely with plastic wrap. Let it rise at room
temperature for at least 1 hour until it has doubled in volume.

COOKING

Preheat the oven to 180°C (350°F/Gas 4). Combine the egg
white and sugar and brush it over the braid. Bake for about
25 minutes until the bread is golden brown. Allow to cool.

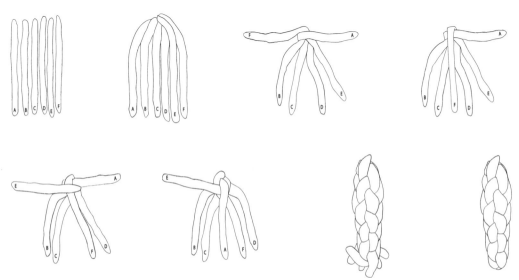

GREEN SMOOTHIE

In New York, Melvin's Juice Box is the place to go for green smoothies. In Paris, it's Bob's Juice Bar and it's J.-P., the manager, who makes them.

SERVES 2
Preparation time: 5 minutes

INGREDIENTS
1 ripe banana, peeled and frozen
250 ml (9 fl oz/1 cup) mineral water
1 huge handful baby spinach
1 tablespoon fresh herbs (mint or parsley)
100 g (3½ oz) frozen mango flesh

Place everything in a blender, ending with the mango so you can adjust the quantity to make up 500 ml (17 fl oz/2 cups), and blend. If your blender isn't powerful enough to handle rock-hard frozen fruit, let the mixture soften for a few minutes before blending.

DOUGHNUTS

There's nothing like a fresh doughnut, like the ones you can get at Doughnut Plant on Manhattan's Lower East Side. Depending on where you live, you might have no choice but to make your own. You'll be glad you did.

MAKES ABOUT 20 DOUGHNUTS

Preparation time: 25 minutes, plus cooling
Resting time: 5½ hours
Cooking time: 2 minutes per doughnut

DOUGH

70 g (2½ oz) coconut oil or
   unsalted butter, melted
350 ml (12 fl oz) milk
820 g (1 lb 13 oz/5⅔ cups)
   plain (all-purpose) flour
3 teaspoons dried yeast
115 g (4 oz) caster (superfine) sugar
2 eggs
1 egg yolk
1½ teaspoons natural vanilla extract
1½ teaspoons fine salt

FRYING

1 litre (35 fl oz/4 cups) oil for frying* (or
   more depending on the size of the pot)

*Check the label on the oil. It
should specifically indicate that the
oil is appropriate for frying.

THE DOUGH

Combine the coconut oil or butter with the milk. Combine the flour with the yeast and sugar. Mix the eggs with the yolk, vanilla and salt. Combine the three mixtures together. Knead until the dough is very elastic (5–10 minutes in a machine, 10–20 minutes by hand). Form a smooth ball of dough, place it in a greased container and cover with plastic wrap. Let it rise at room temperature for about 1½ hours until it has doubled in volume, then refrigerate for at least 3 hours.

SHAPING THE DOUGH

Roll out the dough on a floured surface. Use a cookie cutter to cut out perfectly circular or rectangular shapes. Using a large cookie cutter and a small one for the centre will produce the classic wheel shape of a doughnut. For filled doughnuts (see page 24), the larger circle without a hole cut out is traditional. The dough scraps can be gathered up into a new ball, rerolled and recut one time. To avoid a second lot of scraps, I like to make regular shapes using a pastry cutter, leaving little-to-no excess dough between cuts, or I use the pastry cutter from the get-go to avoid scraps all together. It depends how important the look of the doughnuts is to you. Place each shape on an individual piece of baking paper (otherwise it is difficult to pick up the doughnuts without damaging them when it comes time to fry). Sprinkle flour over to prevent the doughnuts from sticking together, cover loosely with plastic wrap and allow them to rise at room temperature for about 1 hour until they have doubled in volume again.

THE FRYING

Heat the oil in a pot until it reaches 180°C (350°F) or until a cube of bread dropped into the oil turns golden brown in 15 seconds. Using the pieces of baking paper to move the doughnuts, drop two or more at a time into the hot oil. Cook for about 2 minutes on each side until golden. Let the oil reheat for about 30 seconds between batches. Place the hot doughnuts on a wire rack or paper towels to drain excess oil. Allow to cool before glazing (see page 22).

DOUGHNUTS: GLAZES

**EACH GLAZE IS ENOUGH FOR
ABOUT 6 DOUGHNUTS**

HONEY

125 g (4½ oz/1 cup) icing
   (confectioners') sugar, sifted
1 teaspoon acacia or other light honey
40 g (1½ oz) unsalted butter, melted
1½ tablespoons hot water
½ teaspoon natural vanilla extract

VANILLA (WHITE)

175 g (6 oz) icing (confectioners')
   sugar, sifted
1½ tablespoons milk
½ teaspoon natural vanilla extract
Add the milk gradually as you mix.
Add more milk if it's too thick to
dip, but the idea is for the icing
to be as thick as possible so that
it will be opaque when it sets.

MAPLE SYRUP

165 g (5¾ oz/1⅓ cups) icing
   (confectioners') sugar, sifted
45 ml (1½ fl oz) maple syrup
1 pinch salt

CHOCOLATE

25 g (1 oz) unsalted butter, melted
40 g (1½ oz) chocolate, melted
110 g (3¾ oz) icing
   (confectioners') sugar, sifted
2 teaspoons hot water
The butter and chocolate can be
melted together over low heat in
a saucepan or double boiler.

THE GLAZING

For each glaze, simply mix all of the ingredients together in a bowl
with a spoon or fork until combined. Then, holding the doughnuts
in one hand, dip them in the glaze, turning them over the bowl
to allow the excess to drip back into the bowl before placing the
doughnuts on a wire rack to set. A little hot water can be added
to any of the glazes if they have become too thick. If topping with
chopped nuts, do so before the glaze sets to ensure they stick.

DOUGHNUTS: FILLINGS

Doughnuts are often filled with either jam or jelly and dusted with icing sugar — Jelly Doughnuts — or filled with custard and topped with a chocolate glaze — Boston Creams.

FOR 1 DOUGHNUT

1½ tablespoons filling
1 piping (icing) bag

THE TECHNIQUE FOR FILLING A DOUGHNUT

Place the filling (about 1½ tablespoons per doughnut) into a piping (icing) bag fitted with a plain narrow nozzle. Poke a hole in your doughnut using a chopstick or something similar. Insert the nozzle into the hole and gently squeeze the filling into the doughnut. The doughnut will puff up and, when full, the filling will start oozing back out of the hole. In addition to jelly or jam, vanilla custard (vanilla pudding if you eat it on its own) makes a great doughnut filling.

VANILLA CUSTARD

FOR 12 DOUGHNUTS

Preparation time: 15 minutes
Cooking time: 15 minutes

INGREDIENTS

3 teaspoons cornflour (cornstarch)
40 g (1½ oz) sugar
1 pinch salt
210 ml (7½ fl oz) milk
2 egg yolks
25 g (1 oz) unsalted butter
½ vanilla bean, split lengthways
    and seeds scraped

THE MIXTURE

Make a slurry with the cornflour, sugar, salt and about 1 tablespoon of the milk. Mix the egg yolks with the rest of the milk. Combine the two mixtures in a saucepan.

COOKING

Heat over medium heat, whisking constantly. At the first sign of bubbles, remove from the heat but continue to whisk. When the custard starts to get smooth and thick, almost like a mayonnaise, stir in the butter and the scraped vanilla bean and seeds. If the custard needs more cooking to thicken, return the saucepan to a medium heat and stir constantly until thickened.
Tip the custard into a bowl and cover with plastic wrap touching the surface of the cream to prevent a skin from forming.

LEMON POPPY SEED MUFFINS

Of all the muffins we make at Bob's Juice Bar, this is my personal favourite.
J.-P. has been tweaking the recipe for years and they are truly irresistible.

MAKES 12 MUFFINS

Preparation time: 15 minutes, plus cooling
Cooking time: about 25 minutes

DRY INGREDIENTS

320 g (11¼ oz) plain (all-purpose) flour
2 tablespoons + 1 teaspoon poppy seeds
½ teaspoon salt
3 teaspoons baking powder

WET INGREDIENTS

zest of 1 lemon, finely grated
150 g (5½ oz/⅔ cup) caster
    (superfine) sugar
125 g (4½ oz/½ cup) unsalted
    butter, melted
2 eggs
45 ml (1½ fl oz) lemon juice
210 ml (7½ fl oz) yoghurt

FRUIT

100 g (3½ oz) apple, grated
100 g (3½ oz) pear, seeded and diced

GLAZE

125 g (4½ oz/1 cup) icing
    (confectioners') sugar
1½ tablespoons lemon juice
3 teaspoons hot water

THE BATTER

Preheat the oven to 190°C (375°F/Gas 5). Combine all the dry ingredients together. Beat together the wet ingredients. Combine the two mixtures and fold in the fruit.

COOKING

Spoon the batter into a greased 12-hole muffin tin and bake for about 25 minutes until the muffins are golden brown and a skewer inserted into the middle comes out clean. Cool.

THE GLAZING

Mix all of the glaze ingredients in a bowl until combined. Add more water if necessary or if you like a thinner glaze. For a thick white glaze like you see in the photo, don't add too much water — you want to add just enough water for the glaze to be liquid enough to dip the muffins into it. Plunge the head of each muffin into the mixture, allow the excess to drip back into the bowl, then place the muffins on a rack, top side up, and allow the glaze to set.

MANGO LASSI

See recipe page 28.

MANGO LASSI

MAKES 2 LASSIS

Preparation time: 5 minutes

INGREDIENTS

450 g (1 lb) mango flesh
300 g (10½ oz) yoghurt
100 g (3½ oz) ice cubes
1–2 tablespoons honey
seeds of 2 cardamom pods

Set aside 100 g (3½ oz) mango cut into pieces.
Blend all the rest of the ingredients together.
Pour into glasses and add the mango pieces.

BANANA BREAD

A classic cake in the form of a loaf. I like it moist with visible bits of banana and big chunks of chocolate.

MAKES 1 21 X 9 CM (8¼ X 3½ INCH) LOAF

Preparation time: 20 minutes, plus cooling
Cooking time: 55 minutes

DRY INGREDIENTS

165 g (5¾ oz) plain (all-purpose) flour
50 g (1¾ oz) buckwheat flour
1½ teaspoons baking powder
1 teaspoon ground cinnamon

WET INGREDIENTS

60 g (2¼ oz) light brown sugar
70 ml (2¼ fl oz) sunflower oil
2 eggs
175 g (6 oz) sour cream (30% dairy fat)
1 teaspoon natural vanilla extract

FILLINGS

165 g (5¾ oz) banana, finely
   diced or mashed with a fork
110 g (3¾ oz/¾ cup) dark chocolate,
chopped into small pieces

THE BATTER

Preheat the oven to 180°C (350°F/Gas 4). Butter and flour a 21 × 9 cm (8¼ × 3½ inch) loaf (bar) tin. Combine the dry ingredients and beat together the wet ingredients. Stir the banana into the wet mixture and the chocolate into the dry mixture.
Combine the two mixtures without overworking the batter.

COOKING

Fill the tin three-quarters full with the batter. Bake for 45 minutes. Cover with foil and bake for a further 10 minutes. Allow to cool before serving.

note: to make a muffin version of the banana bread, spoon the batter into muffin tins, place a round of banana on top and bake for about 25 minutes at 180°C (350°F/Gas 4). This quantity of mixture makes about 10 muffins.

If you would like to glaze the banana bread as we have done, simply use the glaze recipe on page 26.

STREET FOOD

A huge street food scene which, from the hot dog seller in Central Park to the traditional shaved-ice snow cones on the west side of Brooklyn, reflects a hectic pace of life, an unbridled spirit of enterprise and, more than anything, an insatiable appetite.

BABKA

*This breakfast cake, which looks like a marbled brioche,
is a classic of New York's Jewish bakeries.*

MAKES 1 BABKA
Preparation time: 25 minutes
Resting time: 2½ hours
Cooking time: about 45 minutes

STREUSEL
50 g (1¾ oz) plain (all-purpose) flour
55 g (2 oz) sugar
35 g (1¼ oz) unsalted butter, softened
1 teaspoon ground cinnamon
25 g (1 oz) dark chocolate chips

DRY INGREDIENTS
300 g (10½ oz/2 cups) plain
   (all-purpose) flour
¾ teaspoon dried yeast
2 pinches salt
50 g (1¾ oz) caster (superfine) sugar

WET INGREDIENTS
90 ml (3 fl oz) lukewarm buttermilk
1 egg
1 egg yolk
125 g (4½ oz) unsalted butter, melted
1 egg white, lightly whisked

FILLING
40 g (1¼ oz) cocoa powder
125 g (4½ oz) caster (superfine) sugar
2 teaspoons vanilla sugar
100 g (3½ oz) unsalted
   butter, softened

THE STREUSEL
Make the streusel by mixing all the ingredients together by hand until crumbly. Set aside in the refrigerator for at least 30 minutes.

THE DOUGH
Combine the dry ingredients and beat together the wet ingredients, except the egg white. Combine the two mixtures together. Knead until the dough is very elastic (5–10 minutes in an electric mixer, 10–20 minutes by hand). Form a smooth ball of dough, place it in an oiled container and cover with plastic wrap. Let it rise at room temperature for about 1½ hours until it has doubled in volume.

THE FILLING
Combine the cocoa powder and sugars and set aside.

SHAPING THE DOUGH
On a floured work surface, roll out the dough into a rectangular shape approximately 40 cm (16 inches) long. Spread over the softened butter and sprinkle with the cocoa–sugar mixture. Roll the dough up along its length. Bring the two ends together and twist three times. Butter and flour a 21 × 9 cm (8¼ × 3½ inch) loaf (bar) tin and place the dough twist inside. Cover loosely with plastic wrap and allow it to rise at room temperature for 1 hour until the dough is well risen.

COOKING
Preheat the oven to 180°C (350°F/Gas 4). Brush the surface of the babka with the egg white and scatter over the streusel. Bake for about 45 minutes until golden brown.

COFFEE CAKES

MAKES 14 CAKES

Preparation time: 20 minutes
Refrigeration time: 30 minutes
Cooking time: 35 minutes

STREUSEL

310 g (11 oz) plain (all-purpose) flour
350 g (12 oz) raw (demerara) sugar
220 g (7¾ oz) unsalted butter, softened
3 teaspoons ground cinnamon

WET INGREDIENTS

115 g (4 oz) unsalted butter, softened
200 g (7 oz) caster (superfine) sugar
1 teaspoon natural vanilla extract
2 eggs
160 ml (5¼ fl oz) buttermilk

DRY INGREDIENTS

300 g (10½ oz/2 cups) plain
   (all-purpose) flour
2 teaspoons baking powder
2 pinches salt

INGREDIENTS

220 g (7¾ oz) pear, seeded
   and thinly sliced

THE STREUSEL

Make the streusel by mixing all the ingredients together by hand until crumbly. Set aside in the refrigerator for at least 30 minutes.

THE MIXTURE

Preheat the oven to 180°C (350°F/Gas 4). Beat the butter and sugar vigorously until light and creamy. Mix in the rest of the wet ingredients. Combine the dry ingredients and add to the wet mixture without overworking the batter.

ASSEMBLY AND COOKING

Pour the batter to a depth of 1 cm (½ inch) into 14 buttered and floured round 12 cm (4½ inch) cake tins. Add a few pear slices and top with the streusel just out of the refrigerator (so the streusel holds together better during cooking), without packing it down too much. Bake for 30–35 minutes until a skewer inserted comes out clean.

CINNAMON ROLLS

To fully appreciate these cinnamon rolls, you should eat them just out of the oven, still dripping with cream cheese frosting.

MAKES 10 ROLLS

Preparation time: 30 minutes
Resting time: 2½ hours
Cooking time: about 12 or
    25 minutes (depending on the tin)

DOUGH

400 g (14 oz/2⅔ cups) plain
    (all-purpose) flour
1 teaspoon dried yeast
55 ml (1¾ fl oz) lukewarm water
100 ml (3½ fl oz) lukewarm milk
50 g (1¾ oz) unsalted
    butter, melted
1 egg
2 pinches salt
30 g (1 oz) caster (superfine) sugar
½ teaspoon natural vanilla extract

FILLING

100 g (3½ oz) unsalted
    butter, softened
60 g (2¼ oz) caster (superfine) sugar
4½ teaspoons ground cinnamon
1 tablespoon milk

FROSTING

100 g (3½ oz) icing
    (confectioners') sugar
100 g (3½ oz) plain cream
    cheese, softened
30 ml (1 fl oz) hot water

THE DOUGH

Combine the ingredients for the dough in a mixing bowl, then knead vigorously for 10–15 minutes. Place the dough in an oiled bowl, cover with plastic wrap and let it rest at room temperature for about 1½ hours until the dough has doubled in size.

SHAPING THE DOUGH

On a floured work surface, roll out the dough into a rectangle. Spread over the softened butter and sprinkle with the combined sugar and cinnamon. Roll the dough up along its length if you want to bake the rolls in a large tin, or widthways if you want to bake in individual tins. Cut 10 rolls and place them on a baking tray lined with baking paper or in individual well-buttered tins. Brush with the milk. Cover them loosely with plastic wrap or a clean tea towel (dish towel) and let them rise for 1 hour at room temperature until the dough is well risen.

COOKING

Preheat the oven to 200°C (400°F/Gas 6) and bake the rolls until they're golden brown (allow about 12 minutes for individual rolls and about 25 minutes for a large pan). When they come out of the oven, mix the frosting ingredients together and spread over the rolls while still hot with a spatula or brush. Serve hot if possible.

PECAN ROLLS

This is an upside-down variation of the cinnamon rolls.
These rolls contain pecans and are baked with a caramel topping.

MAKES 10 ROLLS

Preparation time: 30 minutes
Resting time: 2½ hours
Cooking time: about 15 minutes
    + 10 minutes for the pecans

DOUGH

400 g (14 oz/2⅔ cups) plain
    (all-purpose) flour
1 teaspoon dried yeast
55 ml (1¾ fl oz) lukewarm water
100 ml (3½ fl oz) lukewarm milk
50 g (1¾ oz) unsalted
butter, melted
1 egg
2 pinches salt
30 g (1 oz) caster (superfine) sugar
½ teaspoon natural vanilla extract

TOPPING

200 g (7 oz/2 cups) pecans
150 g (5½ oz/¾ cup, lightly
    packed) light brown sugar (or
    140 g/5 oz caster (superfine)
    sugar + 2 teaspoons molasses)
1½ tablespoons maple syrup
60 g (2¼ oz/¼ cup) unsalted
    butter, melted

FILLING

100 g (3½ oz) unsalted
    butter, softened
60 g (2¼ oz) caster (superfine) sugar
½ teaspoon natural vanilla extract

THE DOUGH

Combine the ingredients for the dough in a mixing bowl, then knead vigorously for 10–15 minutes. Place the dough in an oiled bowl, cover with plastic wrap and let it rest at room temperature about 1½ hours until the dough has doubled in size.

THE TOPPING

Preheat the oven to 180°C (350°F/Gas 4). Spread the pecans on a baking tray lined with baking paper and bake for 10 minutes to lightly toast them. Allow to cool.
Butter and flour a 28 × 19 cm (11¼ × 7½ inch) tin. Mix the sugar, maple syrup and melted butter by whisking together until combined and place the pecans and this mixture in the base of the tin.

SHAPING THE DOUGH

On a floured work surface, roll out the dough into a rectangle. Spread over the softened butter and sprinkle with the combined sugar and vanilla. Roll the dough up along its length. Cut 10 rolls and place them on top of the pecan caramel in the tin. Cover loosely with plastic wrap or a clean tea towel (dish towel) and let rise at room temperature for 1 hour until the dough is well risen.

COOKING

Preheat the oven to 200°C (400°F/Gas 6), bake the rolls for about 15 minutes until they are golden brown. Turn them out onto a serving dish; the still-hot caramel will be flowing. Serve hot or lukewarm.

8 : 14

BREAKFAST TIME

BUTTERMILK PANCAKES

Classic pancakes made with buttermilk.

MAKES 7 PANCAKES

Preparation time: 10 minutes
Cooking time: 3–5 minutes per pancake

DRY INGREDIENTS

190 g (6¾ oz) plain (all-purpose) flour
2 pinches bicarbonate of
   soda (baking soda)
2 teaspoons baking powder
3 teaspoons caster (superfine) sugar
½ teaspoon salt

WET INGREDIENTS

210 ml (7½ fl oz) buttermilk
2 eggs
80 g (2¾ oz) unsalted butter, melted
4 drops natural vanilla extract

OTHER INGREDIENTS

blueberries or other fruit (optional)
maple syrup and butter, to serve

THE BATTER

Combine the dry ingredients, beat together the wet ingredients and whisk them into the dry mixture without overworking the batter. The batter should remain lumpy; if you mix until the batter is perfectly smooth, the pancakes may turn out too tough.

COOKING

Heat a frying pan over medium heat with a little oil. I prefer coconut oil, but sunflower oil works as well. Test the frying pan with a small spoonful of batter: if it doesn't sizzle, the pan's not hot enough, if the bottom is too brown before bubbles appear on top, it's too hot. Adjust the heat so that the underside is golden when the top bubbles but isn't dry yet. Pour in a ladle for each pancake and sprinkle with a few blueberries or other fruit if desired. When the underside is golden brown, flip the pancake using a spatula and cook the other side for about 30–40 seconds. Serve hot with maple syrup and butter.

SILVER DOLLAR PANCAKES

Their name comes from the size of a one-dollar coin. Just as with money,
you can never have too many of these super-light pancakes.

MAKES 25 MINI PANCAKES

Preparation time: 10 minutes
Cooking time: 3–5 minutes per pancake

DRY INGREDIENTS

150 g (5½ oz/1 cup) plain
    (all-purpose) flour
1 teaspoon baking powder
1 teaspoon caster (superfine) sugar
1 pinch salt

WET INGREDIENTS

250 ml (9 fl oz/1 cup) milk
2 eggs
25 g (1 oz) unsalted butter, melted
2 drops natural vanilla extract

OTHER INGREDIENTS

maple syrup and butter, to serve

THE BATTER

Combine the dry ingredients, beat together the wet ingredients
and whisk them into the dry mixture without overworking the
batter. The batter should remain lumpy; if you mix until the batter
is perfectly smooth, the pancakes may turn out too tough.

COOKING

Heat a frying pan over medium heat with a little oil. I prefer
coconut oil, but sunflower oil works as well. Test the frying
pan with a small spoonful of batter: if it doesn't sizzle, the
pan's not hot enough, if the bottom is too brown before
bubbles appear on top, it's too hot. Adjust the heat so that the
underside is golden when the top bubbles but isn't dry yet.
Pour in 1 tablespoon for each mini pancake. When the
underside is golden brown, flip the pancake using a
spatula and cook the other side for about 30 seconds.
Serve hot with maple syrup and butter.

CANDIED BACON

See recipe page 88.

CHOCOLATE PROTEIN DRINK

One of J.-P.'s classics at Bob's Juice Bar, this is what I drink to reward myself after a session at the pool.

SERVES 2

Preparation time: 5 minutes

INGREDIENTS

2 bananas, peeled and frozen
1 measure of protein powder
1½ tablespoons cocoa powder
3 teaspoons maple syrup, agave syrup or honey
250 ml (9 fl oz/1 cup) mineral water

Combine all the ingredients together in a blender. You can also use fresh bananas instead of frozen and replace some of the mineral water with ice cubes.

BUCKWHEAT PANCAKES

*My mother likes to start her day with buckwheat pancakes
at Big Nick's Greek diner. This is my dairy-free recipe.*

MAKES 8 PANCAKES

Preparation time: 20 minutes
Cooking time: 3–5 minutes per pancake

DRY INGREDIENTS

125 g (4½ oz) buckwheat flour
125 g (4½ oz) plain (all-purpose) flour
2 teaspoons baking powder
3 teaspoons caster (superfine) sugar
½ teaspoon salt
2 pinches ground cinnamon

WET INGREDIENTS

2 drops natural vanilla extract
1 egg
90 ml (3 fl oz) sunflower oil
350 ml (12 fl oz) water
3 teaspoons baby oat flakes (cooked in
    100 ml (3½ fl oz) water*) or quick oats

OTHER INGREDIENTS

sliced bananas or berries (optional)
    plus extra, to serve
maple syrup and butter, to serve

* Cook the baby oat flakes with the
water in a saucepan over medium heat
for about 5 minutes until the water is
absorbed. Remove from the heat and let
stand for a few minutes until the oats
come away from the base of the pan.

THE BATTER

Combine the dry ingredients, beat together the wet ingredients
and whisk them into the dry mixture without overworking the
batter. The batter should remain lumpy; if you mix until the batter
is perfectly smooth, the pancakes may turn out too tough.

COOKING

Heat a frying pan over medium heat with a little oil. I prefer
coconut oil, but sunflower oil works as well. Test the frying pan
with a small spoonful of batter: if it doesn't sizzle, the pan's not
hot enough, if the bottom is too brown before bubbles appear
on top, it's too hot. Adjust the heat so that the underside is
perfectly golden when the top bubbles but isn't dry yet.
Pour in a ladle for each pancake and sprinkle with berries
or a few slices of banana if using. When the underside
is golden brown, flip the pancake using a spatula and
cook the other side for about 30–40 seconds.
Serve hot with maple syrup, butter and extra fresh fruit.

CHOCOLATE PROTEIN DRINK

See recipe page 48.

PEANUT BUTTER SMOOTHIE

Like the peanut butter and jelly sandwich, this smoothie combines the flavours of berries and peanut butter.

SERVES 2

Preparation time: 5 minutes

INGREDIENTS

1 banana, peeled and frozen
125 g (4½ oz) strawberries, washed, hulled and frozen
2 dried medjool dates, pitted
2 tablespoons peanut butter (page 263)
250 ml (9 fl oz/1 cup)* whatever milk you like
    (almond, rice, cow's, etc.)

* Or enough to make up a total volume of 500 ml
(17 fl oz/2 cups) combined ingredients.

Blend all the ingredients together until you have a creamy mixture. You can also use fresh fruit instead of frozen and replace some of the water with ice cubes.

COCONUT GRANOLA & DRIED MANGO

Eugénie, who helped me make the recipes in this book, makes the best granola I've ever tasted. No exaggeration. This recipe is especially addictive. It's the perfect topping for porridge, an acai cup (see page 256), yoghurt, ice cream …

MAKES 1 SMALL BAKING TRAY OF GRANOLA
Preparation time: 20 minutes, plus cooling
Cooking time: 2 hours 45 minutes

DRIED MANGO
1 mango, ripe but not soft

DRY INGREDIENTS
35 g (1¼ oz) Brazil nuts, roughly chopped
35 g (1¼ oz) cashew nuts,
    roughly chopped
200 g (7 oz/2 cups) large oat
    flakes (rolled oats)
35 g (1¼ oz) unhulled sesame seeds
40 g (1½ oz) desiccated
    (shredded) coconut
40 g (1½ oz/¼ cup) sunflower seeds
35 g (1¼ oz) rice flour
¼ teaspoon salt

INGREDIENTS TO HEAT
70 ml (2¼ fl oz) coconut
    oil or sunflower oil
1 tablespoon raw (demerara) sugar
150 g (5½ oz) honey
1 teaspoon natural vanilla extract

DRIED MANGO
Preheat the oven to 90°C (200°F/Gas ½). Cut the mango into slices about 5 mm (¼ inch) thick and lay them flat on a baking tray lined with baking paper, making sure they don't overlap or touch. Place in the oven for about 45 minutes. Turn them over, then continue baking for a further 45 minutes. Allow them to cool and then lay them flat in an airtight container between layers of baking paper so they don't stick together.

THE GRANOLA
Preheat the oven to 150°C (300°F/Gas 2).
Combine all the dry ingredients in a bowl.
In a large saucepan, heat the coconut oil, sugar, honey and vanilla over medium heat, whisking constantly. Remove from the heat when the mixture starts to boil. Immediately pour over the dry ingredients and mix together carefully with a spatula. When the mixture is evenly coated, pour it onto a baking tray lined with baking paper and spread out into a layer about 1.5 cm (⅝ inch) thick.

COOKING AND SERVING
Bake for about 40 minutes, checking its progress at regular intervals. If the granola is browning too quickly, reduce the oven temperature to 140°C (275°F/Gas 1) and cover the granola with a sheet of foil. When it starts to dry out and form clumps, remove the tray from the oven and stir gently with a spatula. Return to the oven for 20–30 minutes. Cut up the mango slices if you need to and mix them into the granola, then return to the oven for 10 minutes. Allow to cool at room temperature before breaking the granola into pieces. The granola will keep for at least 3 weeks in an airtight container at room temperature.

note: you can store the dried mangoes for 1 month in an airtight container away from heat and moisture. They will stay soft and retain a melt-in-the-mouth texture.

tip: depending on your taste, you can add shaved dried coconut and fresh banana slices when serving.

HOT OATMEAL

A healthy alternative when you're looking for a comforting hot breakfast treat.

SERVES 2

Preparation time: 10 minutes
Cooking time: 5 minutes

INGREDIENTS

120 g (4¼ oz) baby oat
 flakes or quick oats
550–600 ml (19–21 fl oz)
 milk or water
½ teaspoon salt
3 teaspoons light brown sugar,
 honey or agave syrup (optional)
½ teaspoon ground cinnamon
 or natural vanilla extract
2 teaspoons butter or peanut butter

PREPARATION

Combine all the ingredients, except the butter or peanut butter, in a saucepan and cook over medium heat, stirring. After about 5 minutes, when it is good and thick, turn off the heat, add the butter or peanut butter and let it sit for about 1 minute so that the porridge can set and come away from the base of the pan.

SERVING

Serve hot with fresh fruit, granola, the warm milk of your choice (cow's, soy, almond, etc.), seeds and the sweetener of your choice (light brown sugar, maple syrup, honey, etc.).

PEANUT BUTTER SMOOTHIE

See recipe page 52.

BAGEL

See recipe page 72.

UPPER WEST SIDE

Located in the north-west of Manhattan, this neighbourhood is a paradise for food lovers, with Greek restaurants like Tom's Restaurant, the Broadway Restaurant and Big Nick's, kosher delis like Barney Greengrass and Murray's Sturgeon Shop, and two of New York's best markets: Fairway and Zabar's.

DINER

FILET OF MATJES HERRING
3 19 EA.

MURRAY'S FILET OF PICKLED HERRING IN CLEAR
3.49 EA.

MURRAY'S FILET OF SCHMALTZ HERRING
3.9 9 EA.

BEEFBURGER
Onion · Cole Slaw · Pickle 5.05
BEEFBURGER Deluxe
French Fries · Lettuce · Tomato 6.65
Cole Slaw · Pickle
CHEESEBURGER
Onion · Cole Slaw · Pickle 5.45
CHEESEBURGER DeLuxe
French Fries · Lettuce · Tomato 7.10
Cole Slaw · Pickle
BACON BURGER 5.65
BACON BURGER De Luxe
French Fries · Lettuce · Tomato 7.25
Cole Slaw · Pickle
BACON CHEESEBURGER 6.05
BACON CHEESEBURGER DeLuxe
French Fries · Lettuce · Tomato 7.65
Slaw · Pickle

2 EGGS Any Style
POTATOES & TOAST
2 EGGS Any Style
BACON, HAM or SAUSAGE
POTATOES & TOAST
1 EGG BACON, HAM or SAUSAGE ANY STYLE
CORNED BEEF HASH
2 EGG, POTATOES & TOAST
PANCAKES with Syrup & Butter
with BACON, HAM or SAUSAGE
FRENCH TOAST Syrup & Butter
with BACON, HAM or SAUSAGE

6.35 VIRGINIA
with 2 EGGS Potatoes & Toast
6.05 SHELL STEAK
with 2 EGGS Potatoes & Toast
6.35 PASTRAMI & 2 EGGS
with POTATOES & TOAST
5.25 SALAMI & 2 EGGS
with POTATOES & TOAST
6.75
5.25
6.75

Magnets $3.00

THE RESTAURANT
TOM'S RESTAURANT

MATZAH BREI

This is how my grandmother made this traditional recipe that's like a scrambled French toast made from matzo crackers. It is eaten especially during Pesach (Passover) to celebrate the emancipation of the slaves. Power to the people!

SERVES 2

Preparation time: 15 minutes
Cooking time: 10 minutes

INGREDIENTS

300 g (10½ oz) matzo crackers
4 eggs
125 ml (4 fl oz/½ cup) milk
½ teaspoon ground cinnamon
1 pinch salt
1 teaspoon sugar
40 g (1½ oz) butter
2 tablespoons neutral cooking oil

PREPARATION

With your hands, break the matzo crackers up into bite-sized pieces. Soak the broken matzo in cold water for 5 minutes. While the matzo is soaking, combine the other ingredients, except the butter and oil, in a bowl, mixing with a fork or whisk. Drain the soaked matzo in a colander, then place it in the egg–milk batter and let it soak until most or all of the mixture has been absorbed. Drain off any excess liquid in a colander.

COOKING

In a frying pan, heat the butter and oil over medium heat — you want enough to just cover the surface. When the butter and oil start to sizzle, add the matzo, spreading it out so the matzo is no more than one or two layers thick. Depending on the size of your pan, you may need to cook it in batches. Flip and separate the matzo so it's slightly golden and scrambled on both sides. This takes about 5 minutes. Serve hot with jam or other sweet toppings. Personally, I like to mix in obscene amounts of jam.

CHOCOLATE RUGELACHS

You'll enjoy making these cute little twists as much as eating them.

MAKES 12 CRESCENTS

Preparation time: 30 minutes, plus cooling
Resting time: 4 hours
Cooking time: about 20 minutes

DOUGH

95 g (3¼ oz) plain (all-purpose) flour
60 g (2¼ oz/¼ cup) plain
    cream cheese, softened
60 g (2¼ oz/¼ cup) unsalted
    butter, softened
2 pinches salt

GANACHE

30 ml (1 fl oz) thin (pouring) cream
2 teaspoons unsalted butter
60 g (2¼ oz) dark chocolate,
    broken into pieces

TOPPING

50 g (1¾ oz) dark chocolate,
    finely chopped
50 g (1¾ oz) caster (superfine) sugar

GLAZE

1 egg yolk
1 teaspoon water

TOPPING (JAM VERSION)

3 teaspoons sugar
1 teaspoon ground cinnamon (optional)

THE DOUGH

Using a food processor or by hand, mix the dough ingredients until combined. Wrap in plastic wrap and refrigerate for at least 4 hours.

THE GANACHE

In a saucepan, heat the cream and butter over medium heat until they come to the boil. Add the pieces of chocolate. Take off the heat and let it melt for 1 minute. Stir with a spatula until smooth and even.

SHAPING THE DOUGH

Preheat the oven to 170°C (325°F/Gas 3). On a floured work surface, roll out the dough with a rolling pin to make a round about 30 cm (12 inches) in diameter. Spread the ganache with a spatula over the whole round. Mix together the topping ingredients and scatter over the ganache, setting some aside for sprinkling on top. Cut the round into 12 equal wedges, like a pie, and roll each one up, starting with the wider end, to make a small crescent. Place the completed crescents, as you make them, on a baking tray lined with baking paper.

THE GLAZING

Brush the rugelachs with the mixture of egg yolk and water. Sprinkle over the reserved chocolate–sugar topping.

COOKING

Bake in the oven for about 20 minutes until the crescents are golden brown. Allow to cool for at least 10 minutes before serving.

TO MAKE JAM RUGELACHS

Replace the ganache and chocolate topping with 165 g (5¾ oz/½ cup) jam (apricot or raspberry work well) and 80 g (2¾ oz) nuts (pine nuts or pistachios, depending on your taste) and sprinkle the rugelachs with the mixture of sugar and cinnamon.

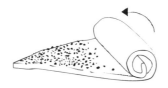

FRENCH TOAST

French toast is one of the first things I learned to cook as a child. When I would go to a diner with my mother for breakfast, she would always ask them to make it well soaked.

SERVES 2

Preparation time: 10 minutes
Cooking time: 5 minutes

INGREDIENTS

300 g (10½ oz) challah (page 14)
4 eggs
70 ml (2¼ fl oz) milk
70 ml (2¼ fl oz) thin (pouring) cream
3 drops natural vanilla extract
½ teaspoon ground cinnamon
1 pinch salt
2 teaspoons sugar
40 g (1½ oz) butter or 2 tablespoons
   neutral cooking oil
maple syrup and butter, to serve

PREPARATION

Cut the challah into 2–3 cm (¾–1¼ inch) slices.
The loaf can be fresh, but slightly stale is even better.
Mix all of the other ingredients, except the butter
or oil, with a fork or a whisk until combined.
Soak the bread in this mixture for a few minutes
on each side until the slices are fully saturated.

COOKING AND SERVING

Brown the soaked slices in a frying pan over
medium heat in the butter or oil for 2–3 minutes
each side. The slices should be golden on
the outside but still moist on the inside.
Serve with maple syrup and butter.

*tip: in my opinion, French toast made with challah is the
best, but a good sandwich bread or brioche works well.*

RICE CRISPY TREATS

This all-American classic was invented by Kellogg's® and is usually made using Rice Krispies® and industrial marshmallows. Making them with home-made marshmallows and organic puffed rice are two ways to improve on the original.

MAKES 16 SQUARES

Preparation time: 10 minutes, plus cooling
Cooking time: 5 minutes

INGREDIENTS

70 g (2½ oz) unsalted butter
600 g (1 lb 5 oz) marshmallow (page 232)
2 pinches salt
350 g (12 oz) puffed rice (Rice Krispies®, Rice Bubbles® or other)

THE MIXTURE

Oil or butter a square 24 cm (9½ inch) cake tin.
Melt the butter, marshmallow and salt in a pan over low heat. Be careful not to overcook the mixture; stop the cooking as soon as the butter and marshmallow have melted. Mix the melted marshmallow and butter with the puffed rice in a large bowl.

SETTING AND SERVING

Using a spatula, transfer everything to the tin, pressing just enough to get the mixture well distributed but being careful not to crush the puffed rice.
Allow to cool and cut into squares.

tip: you can also add twists to this recipe, like chocolate chips, seeds or nuts.

BLINTZ

I used to devour these Ashkenazi-style filled crêpes at my grandmother's in Brooklyn.
My two favourite fillings were cheese and blueberries.

MAKES 12 BLINTZ

Preparation time: 30 minutes
Resting time: 1 hour
Cooking time: 40 minutes

DRY INGREDIENTS

250 g (9 oz/1⅔ cups) plain
    (all-purpose) flour
3 pinches salt
2 teaspoons caster (superfine) sugar

WET INGREDIENTS

300 ml (10½ fl oz) milk
200 ml (7 fl oz) water
50 g (1¾ oz) unsalted
    butter, melted
4 eggs

CHEESE FILLING

450 g (1 lb) ricotta cheese
100 g (3½ oz) caster
    (superfine) sugar
3 egg whites
4½ teaspoons cornflour (cornstarch)

BLUEBERRY FILLING

30 g (1 oz) unsalted butter
500 g (1 lb 2 oz) blueberries
85 g (3 oz) caster (superfine) sugar
4½ teaspoons cornflour (cornstarch)
sour cream, for topping

THE BATTER

Combine the dry ingredients. Whisk together the wet ingredients vigorously, then add the dry mixture while beating until combined. You need to let the batter rest for at least 1 hour before cooking. If possible, make it the night before and keep it in the refrigerator.

THE CHEESE FILLING

Combine the ingredients for the cheese filling with a fork. Cook the filling in a saucepan over low heat, stirring constantly for 10 minutes or until you have a consistency similar to mashed potato.

THE BLUEBERRY FILLING

Melt the butter in a pan over medium heat. Combine the blueberries, sugar and cornflour and cook in the butter for 5 minutes or until it has thickened.

COOKING AND SERVING

Heat a little oil in a frying pan over medium heat. Pour and spread a ladle of batter in the hot frying pan. When the bottom begins to brown, turn the pancake with a spatula. Spread about 2 tablespoons of filling in the middle of the crêpe, fold in the edges and roll the crêpe to enclose the filling. Keep cooking the blintz on both sides — it should be golden brown all over. Serve hot with sour cream.

11 : 28

BRUNCH TIME

BAGELS

This iconic wheel-shaped bread was first brought to New York by Jewish immigrants from Eastern Europe. Authentic, fresh, bagels are still quite rare outside of New York, which is why some of us like to make our own.

MAKES 10 BAGELS

Preparation time: 40 minutes
Resting time: 1 hour
Cooking time: 45 minutes

DRY INGREDIENTS

750 g (1 lb 10 oz/5 cups)
    strong flour
1½ teaspoons dried yeast
3 teaspoons salt

WET INGREDIENTS

375 ml (13 fl oz/1½ cups) lukewarm
    water (or 400 ml/14 fl oz if you
    add the wheat gluten, see note)
2 tablespoons malt syrup
    or sugar syrup
1½ tablespoons olive oil

POACHING INGREDIENTS

3 teaspoons potato starch
3 litres (105 fl oz/12 cups) water
3 teaspoons malt syrup
    or sugar syrup
1½ teaspoons salt

TOPPING (OPTIONAL)

sesame seeds and poppy seeds are
    the most traditional, but you can
    experiment with other things

THE DOUGH

Combine the dry ingredients and beat together the wet ingredients. Combine the two mixtures and knead vigorously for about 10 minutes until the dough is smooth and elastic. Divide the dough into 10 equal portions and form into small balls.

SHAPING THE DOUGH

Using the palms of your hands, flatten and stretch the balls of dough to make sausages 20–25 cm (8–10 inches) long. Flatten one of the ends into a hook shape. Wrap it around the other end and pinch to seal.
Place each bagel on an individual square of baking paper to make it easier to move them later. Scatter over some flour, then cover with plastic wrap and allow them to rise at room temperature for 1 hour.

COOKING

Preheat the oven to 230°C (450°F/Gas 8). If it is an electric oven, place a bowl of water in the bottom of the oven 15 minutes before baking.
Blend the potato starch into 250 ml (9 fl oz/1 cup) of the cold water, then dissolve it with the rest of the poaching ingredients in a large saucepan. Bring to a rolling boil and then lower the heat so the water is just simmering. Drop the bagels into the water, in batches if necessary. After about 1 minute, turn them over and cook for another 30 seconds. Take them out using a slotted spoon and place them on a baking tray lined with baking paper. Finally, sprinkle the topping over the damp bagels.
Place the tray of bagels in the oven, lower the temperature to 210°C (415°F/Gas 6–7) and bake for 20–25 minutes until the bagels start to brown.

note: if you can't find strong flour, which is a high protein (high gluten) flour, you can use plain flour with the addition of 1½ tablespoons wheat gluten (available from health food stores).

CHICKEN SALAD SANDWICH

This has a traditional Mexican avocado spread which replaces the usual mayonnaise in a chicken salad.

MAKES 2 SANDWICHES
Preparation time: 15 minutes

SANDWICHES
2 bagels (page 72)

GUACAMOLE
1 small ripe avocado, halved,
   stone removed and peeled
40 g (1½ oz) red onion,
   finely chopped
½ lime
2 pinches salt + 1 turn of
   the pepper mill
1 pinch ground cumin
1–2 drops of Tabasco®
   sauce (optional)

FILLING
300 g (10½ oz) leftover roast
   chicken (page 142)
4 slices of tomato
1 handful rocket (arugula)
2 pinches salt + 2 turns
   of the pepper mill

THE GUACAMOLE
Crush the avocado with a fork. Add the chopped red onion to the mashed avocado, squeeze the half lime and add the juice to the mixture. Season with the salt and pepper and add the cumin and Tabasco® sauce, if using.

THE FILLING AND ASSEMBLY
Chop the leftover chicken into small pieces. Add them to the guacamole. Combine gently.
Slice the bagels in half horizontally, then top the bottom half of each bagel with the chicken–guacamole mixture. Add two slices of tomato to each sandwich and divide the handful of greens. Season with the salt and pepper. Cover with the top half of the bagel and enjoy immediately.

DILL POTATO SALAD
See recipe page 114.

SMOKED SALMON BAGEL

The classic New York breakfast sandwich as sold at fine establishments like Murray's Sturgeon Shop on the Upper West Side of Manhattan. Nothing can beat it!

MAKES 2 SANDWICHES

Preparation time: 5 minutes

INGREDIENTS

2 bagels (page 72)
80 g (2¾ oz) plain cream cheese
 (e.g. Philadelphia®, St Môret®)
200 g (7 oz) smoked salmon
2 slices white onion (optional)
6 thin slices of tomato

Slice the bagels in half horizontally. You can
toast them if you want to, but normally, if
they are fresh, it's not worth the trouble.
Spread both halves with a thick layer of cream cheese
and, on the bottom half, add in order: smoked
salmon, one slice white onion, if using, and two
or three thin slices of tomato. Top with the other
half of the bagel and cut in two before serving.

BIALYS

While the bagel is boiled and baked, its lesser known cousin, the bialy,
is just baked. The other big difference is that the bialy only has a hollow
in the middle while the bagel has a hole.

MAKES 6 BIALYS

Preparation time: 25 minutes
Resting time: 2½ hours
Cooking time: 15 minutes

DOUGH

400 g (14 oz/2⅔ cups) strong flour
1½ teaspoons dried yeast
3 teaspoons salt
250 ml (9 fl oz/1 cup)
    lukewarm water
3 teaspoons olive oil

COOKING TRAY

1 small knob of butter
2 pinches fine polenta (cornmeal)

FILLING

1½ tablespoons olive oil
150 g (5½ oz) onion,
    finely chopped
1 teaspoon poppy seeds
1 teaspoon salt

THE DOUGH

Mix together the flour, yeast and salt. In a bowl, beat the
lukewarm water and olive oil. Incorporate the first mixture into
the second and knead vigorously by hand or using an electric
mixer for 10 minutes until the dough is smooth and elastic.
Form a smooth ball of dough. Place the dough in an oiled bowl,
cover with plastic wrap and let it rest at room temperature
for about 1½ hours until the dough has doubled in size.

SHAPING THE DOUGH

Divide the dough into six equal portions. Shape into small
balls and flatten them between the palms of your hands.
Place the rounds of dough on a buttered and floured sheet of
baking paper. Fold the opposite edges of each dough portion
towards the middle and pinch together to make irregular
balls. Sprinkle with flour, then cover loosely with plastic wrap.
Let them rise at room temperature for at least 1 hour.
Using the palm of your hand, flatten the risen balls of dough,
then press the middle of each bialy to make a large hollow.

THE FILLING

Heat the olive oil in a frying pan and sauté the onions and
poppy seeds over medium heat. Season with the salt.
Put a little of the onion–poppy seed mixture in the middle of each
bialy and brush the surface of the bialys with more olive oil. Don't
worry if the onion mixture spills out, bialys should be imperfect!

COOKING

Preheat the oven to 220°C (425°F/Gas 7). Grease a baking
tray with the butter and sprinkle with the polenta. Place
the bialys in the middle or upper part of the oven and bake
for about 10 minutes until they're lightly browned.

MACKEREL BIALYS

In New York, this sandwich filling is made using white fish, but in France I use smoked mackerel, which is technically a 'blue' fish. I can guarantee it's just as good.

MAKES 3 BIALYS
Preparation time: 20 minutes
Refrigeration time: at least
   30 minutes

SANDWICHES
3 bialys (page 78)

FILLING
150 g (5½ oz) smoked, cooked blue
   fish (mackerel or 'bloater' herring)
50 g (1¾ oz) fennel and/or
   celery, finely chopped
25 g (1 oz) onion, finely chopped
2 tablespoons sour cream
1 tablespoon plain
   mayonnaise (page 264)
1 pinch salt + 1 turn of
   the pepper mill

ASSEMBLY
6 lettuce leaves (cos/romaine
   or butter lettuce)
½ Lebanese (short) cucumber, sliced
   very thinly or the equivalent
   amount of sweet pickles (see
   'fast pickles', page 242)

THE FILLING
Remove the skin from the fish and lift the flesh from the bones. Add the fennel and/or celery, onion, sour cream and mayonnaise. Season with the salt and pepper and gently combine. Place in the refrigerator for at least 30 minutes.

THE ASSEMBLY
Slice the bialys in two. Cover the bottom half of each bialy with two lettuce leaves, then add the blue fish filling. Top with the slices of cucumber or pickle and the other half of each bialy. Enjoy immediately.

COLESLAW
See recipe page 265.

TAKE A NUMBER

KATZ'S

In the 1930s, the golden age of Yiddish theatre in Manhattan's Lower East Side, this Jewish delicatessen was the place to be seen. Today, with its inimitable corned beef sandwiches and its knishes, it remains an indispensable institution for locals and tourists alike.

EGGS OVER EASY

*These are sunny-side up eggs
that are briefly flipped over.*

SERVES 1

Preparation time: 5 minutes
Cooking time: 5 minutes

INGREDIENTS

2½ tablespoons unsalted butter or olive oil
2 eggs

THE EGGS

Heat the butter or olive oil, or a combination of
the two, over medium heat in a (truly) non-stick
frying pan. When the butter or olive oil starts to
sizzle, carefully crack the eggs into the frying pan.
After a couple of minutes, use a wide, thin, clean
spatula to make sure that the eggs are completely
unstuck from the bottom of the frying pan, gently
sliding it under the eggs to loosen any sticky
spots. Now tilt the pan to slide an egg onto the
spatula (jiggling the spatula forward if necessary)
and then gently flip the egg over at the edge of
the frying pan (don't drop it!). Repeat with the
other egg. After 20 seconds or so, tilt the pan to
slide the eggs onto the edge of a plate. Season.
If you practise enough, making eggs this way will
eventually come naturally. Along the way, you can
consider eggs over easy as an exercise in gentleness.

PAN-FRIED BACON

See recipe page 88.

HASH BROWNS

See recipe page 86.

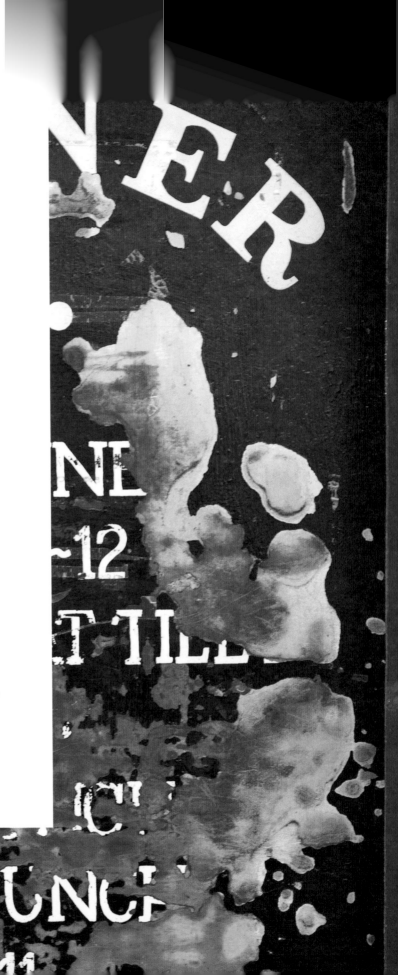

HASH BROWNS

Pan-fried grated potatoes.

SERVES 2

Preparation time: 10 minutes
Cooking time: 20 minutes

INGREDIENTS

400 g (14 oz) russet or sebago
    potatoes (about 2 large potatoes)
200 ml (7 fl oz) cooking oil

PREPARING THE POTATOES

Peel the potatoes and grate them with a hand grater or
the grater attachment of a food processor. Over a sieve
(to catch any pieces that fall), squeeze the potatoes
by hand to extract as much water as possible.

COOKING

To a small frying pan over medium heat, add enough oil
to come to 5 mm (¼ inch) and heat until sizzling. Add
enough potato to completely fill the frying pan with a layer
about 1 cm (½ inch) thick. The exact amount will depend
on the size of the frying pan. Use a spatula to spread out the
potato evenly, then gently push down on the edge of the
potato, which naturally contract to a semi-solid pancake.
After about 5 minutes, when the underside is golden brown,
use a wide spatula to flip the potato over. The smaller the frying
pan, the more likely you will be able to flip all of the potato
in one piece. Continue cooking for a further 5 minutes until
the second side of the hash brown is golden brown. Place
the hash brown on paper towels or a wire rack to drain off
excess oil, then repeat with the remaining potato and oil.

SERVING

You can keep the hash browns warm in an oven preheated
to 100°C (200°F/Gas ½). Season with salt and pepper.

CHARCOAL PRIME STEAKS & RIBS

DISCOVER MasterCard VISA AMERICAN EXPRESS

BIG NICK'S JOINTS HAVE BEEN FEATURE[D]
- DAILY NEWS | • ABC-TV NEWS • N.Y. TIM[ES]
- NEW YORK | • NEW. DA[ILY]
  MAG.(GAEL GREENE) | • WOR-RADIO | • WESTSI[DE]
- GOOD | (JOAN HAMEURG)
  HOUSEK'G | • NY ON $60 A DAY. • "MIDNIGH[T]
- TV SHOW[S] | COW[BOY]

SMOKED BACON

I love smoked bacon in the morning. The smell alone (especially when combined with coffee) is reason enough to wake up. And somehow it just seems to blend perfectly with whatever else I'm having for breakfast — whether it's something purely savoury like eggs and potatoes, or something sweeter like pancakes or French toast, where my favourite thing is to let the crispy, salty bacon steep in the maple syrup. I like to cook it a few different ways but, regardless of method, I would advise you to get the best quality meat you can afford, as it will make all the difference.

PAN-FRIED BACON

This is the method I use when I'm making bacon for just a few people or when using an oven is impractical.

Lay the strips of bacon side by side in a cold non-stick frying pan. Heat over medium heat and after a few minutes, when the bacon naturally comes unstuck from the base of the pan, turn the slices using chopsticks or tongs. Continue cooking and turning until the bacon is as crispy as you like it. Drain on paper towels and serve.

OVEN-BAKED BACON

This is a better method if you need to make a lot of bacon in one shot. The crispness of the bacon is also more even, and it's not as messy as cooking it in the frying pan.

Preheat the oven to 200°C (400°F/Gas 6). Place the slices of bacon side by side on a baking tray (lined with baking paper or unlined). Bake for about 15 minutes until the bacon is as crispy as you like it.

CANDIED BACON

Oven-baked bacon with an indulgent twist.

Preheat the oven to 160°C (315°F/Gas 2–3). Line a baking tray with baking paper. Pour some caster (superfine) sugar onto a wide plate. Coat the bacon with the sugar by laying it on the sugar on the plate, one strip at a time, and flipping it over with your fingers. Lay the sugar-coated strips of bacon on the baking paper and bake for 25–30 minutes, checking regularly that the sugar isn't burning. Serve hot or warm.

HUEVOS RANCHEROS

In Brooklyn, you can find an excellent rendition of this Mexican breakfast dish at one of the La Esquina restaurants. To recreate an authentic experience in Paris, I turned to my personal expert on all things Mexican, who also happens to be my business partner, Amaury de Veyrac.

SERVES 2

Preparation time: 45 minutes
Cooking time: 35 minutes

TORTILLAS (MAKES 10)

150 g (5½ oz/1 cup) plain
   (all-purpose) flour
150 g (5½ oz) fine polenta
   (cornmeal) or replace with the
   same quantity of wheat flour
200 ml (7 fl oz) lukewarm water

TOMATO SALSA

1 small red onion, finely chopped
2 tomatoes, seeded and chopped
1 pinch dried oregano
1 teaspoon sugar
1 garlic clove, finely chopped
1 jalapeño pepper or 1 pinch
Espelette chilli powder

EGGS AND TOPPING

4 tablespoons tinned black
   beans, rinsed (optional)
1 pinch salt
2 eggs
100 g (3½ oz) emmental
   cheese, finely grated
1 lime
1 avocado, chopped (optional)
4 sprigs coriander (cilantro),
   roughly chopped

THE TORTILLA DOUGH

Combine the flour and polenta in a bowl. Add the water gradually while working the mixture until you have a firm dough. Continue to knead the dough at length on a floured surface. When you have a ball of dough that's nice and smooth, divide it into 10 equal portions and roll them out on the floured surface, making the tortillas as thin as possible.

COOKING THE TORTILLAS

Heat a non-stick frying pan over high heat and cook the tortillas for about 1 minute on each side. You should have some brown marks on both sides. Stack the ones that are ready between two sheets of foil to prevent them from drying out.

THE TOMATO SALSA

Lightly sauté the onion in a saucepan in a little sunflower oil over medium heat. Add the remaining ingredients, season with salt and pepper, then reduce the heat to low. Cover and cook, stirring occasionally, for 15 minutes. Place in a food processor or blender and process until a chunky salsa forms.

EGGS AND TOPPING

If you choose the black beans option, heat them up with the salt in a saucepan, then mash them with a fork. Keep them warm in the oven, covered.
Fry two to four tortillas (depending on how hungry you are) with sunflower oil in a frying pan over high heat for about 2 minutes on each side (you can freeze the others, wrapped in plastic wrap). Fry the eggs in the same frying pan and scatter over three-quarters of the cheese. Juice the lime.

ASSEMBLY

On each plate, place the egg on the warm tortilla with the tomato salsa (around the yolk), a few pieces of avocado, if using, the mashed black beans, if using, chopped coriander, the rest of the cheese and a little lime juice. *Buen provecho!*

OMELETTE

What I like in an omelette is a soft tubular form (not just a circle folded in half), a moist yellow (not dry and grilled) surface and a slightly wet (but not uncooked) interior. After this, there is no limit to what can go inside.

MAKES 1 OMELETTE
Preparation time: 10 minutes
Cooking time: 20 minutes

FILLING
2 knobs of butter
1 large handful baby spinach
1 large handful mushrooms, sliced
3 teaspoons pine nuts
60 g (2¼ oz/½ cup) goat's
    cheese, crumbled

OMELETTE
3 or 4 eggs
1 tablespoon milk
1 pinch salt
1 teaspoon dried herbs or fresh
    herbs, chopped (optional)
40 g (1½ oz) butter or
    2 tablespoons sunflower oil

THE FILLING
This is a filling that I often make at home: baby spinach with pine nuts, goat's cheese and fried mushrooms.
Heat the butter in a frying pan over medium heat, then sweat the spinach and brown the mushrooms separately, discarding the liquid released from the vegetables each time. When cooked place them in a bowl together. Toast the pine nuts for 1–2 minutes until golden and add to the mushrooms and spinach. Add the crumbled goat's cheese.

THE OMELETTE
Whisk together all the omelette ingredients, except the butter or oil, until all of the ingredients are very well combined.
Melt the butter or oil over low–medium heat in a non-stick frying pan and pour in the eggs. It is absolutely essential that the eggs not stick to the bottom of the frying pan, which is why I advise a generous portion of butter or oil, and insist on a truly non-stick frying pan. But feel free to cut down on the fat if you know that your pan doesn't need it.
Using a spatula, move the eggs in a folding motion almost as if making scrambled eggs, tilting the frying pan as you do this so that liquid egg will fill in the empty spaces created by the spatula. The idea is to evenly cook the eggs on a low–medium heat so you don't have an omelette that's overcooked (too dark) on the outside and/or undercooked inside. After a few minutes, when the eggs have mostly thickened but are still visibly wet, tilt the frying pan one last time to fill any holes and add your filling in a strip across the omelette, at about the one-third mark of the omelette circle.

THE FOLDING
Allow the eggs to set for a minute or so before using the spatula to check whether they're cooked enough to hold together when folding. When this is the case (before the eggs have dried out), fold the omelette around the filling to form a tube and slide onto a plate.

HASH BROWNS
See recipe page 86.

EGGS BENEDICT

Legend has it that a guest at the Waldorf Astoria hotel in New York invented eggs Benedict in the hope of easing his hangover. While off-the-shelf hollandaise sauces are readily available, I encourage you to make your own. It will make all the difference.

SERVES 6

Preparation time: 20 minutes
Cooking time: 25 minutes

HOLLANDAISE SAUCE

2 egg yolks
1 teaspoon lemon juice
1 teaspoon white wine
115 g (4 oz) unsalted butter
   (preferably clarified), melted

EGGS

12 eggs
white vinegar or rice vinegar
12–24 bacon slices
6 English muffins (page 96)
100 g (3½ oz) butter
cayenne pepper (optional)

THE SAUCE

Bring a saucepan of water to the boil and turn off the heat. In a large bowl, whisk the egg yolks, lemon juice and wine (or water) until the mixture has thickened noticeably. Place the bowl over the saucepan of hot water and slowly pour in the melted butter while whisking constantly to form an emulsion that should be a bit less thick than a mayonnaise. Keep the bowl over the warm water until you're ready to serve. If the sauce becomes too thick, whisk in a little hot water to thin it out.

THE POACHED EGGS

If you don't have an egg poacher, you can poach your eggs the old-fashioned way. Bring 1–2 litres (35–70 fl oz/4–8 cups) of water to the boil in a large saucepan, then turn the heat down to a simmer. Add a little vinegar to help the eggs coagulate (1–2 tablespoons per litre of water). Carefully break an egg into a small cup or bowl and slide it slowly into the water — the aim being to keep the egg white from spreading all over the place. Use a spatula to nudge the white around the yolk. When the white is set (i.e. no longer transparent), but before it is hard and pale, remove the poached egg with a slotted spoon. Poached eggs that are not being served immediately can be removed from the water slightly undercooked and kept in a bowl of iced water until ready to serve. They can then be reheated in gently simmering water for about 20 seconds.

THE MEAT

Round, so-called 'Canadian', bacon is traditional, but feel free to use any other cured meats, such as smoked bacon or coppa. In any case, brown it in a frying pan over medium heat for a few minutes on each side until it is as crispy as you like it. Another popular twist is to replace the meat with a mixture of smoked salmon and cooked spinach.

ASSEMBLY

Toast the English muffins and spread with butter. Lay one or two slices of bacon on top, then the eggs. Pour over some sauce and sprinkle with cayenne pepper.

POTATOES

See 'home fries' recipe page 265.

ENGLISH MUFFINS

My baker friend Gavin Smart was kind enough to share his recipe for English muffins.

MAKES 10 MUFFINS
Preparation time: 30 minutes
Resting time: about 3 hours
Cooking time: 30 minutes

LIQUID LEVAIN
MAKES 3 PORTIONS
Preparation time: 20 minutes
Resting time: about 2½ days

PREPARATION 1
55 ml (1¾ fl oz) lukewarm water
50 g (1¾ oz/⅓ cup) wholemeal
    (whole-wheat) flour

PREPARATION 2
100 ml (3½ fl oz) water
100 g (3½ oz/⅔ cup) strong flour
1 tablespoon caster (superfine) sugar

PREPARATION 3
200 g (7 oz/1⅓ cups) strong flour
200 ml (7 fl oz) water

INGREDIENTS
30 g (1 oz) sugar
455 ml (16 fl oz) water (at
    around 40°C/105°F)
30 g (1 oz) fresh yeast
1 portion (235 g/8½ oz)
    liquid levain
875 g–1 kg (1 lb 15 oz–2 lb
    4 oz) strong flour
60 g (2¼ oz) milk powder
60 g (2¼ oz/¼ cup) unsalted
    butter, softened
3 teaspoons salt
semolina flour, for dusting

THE LIQUID LEVAIN

Whisk together the ingredients for the first preparation in a bowl, cover with plastic wrap and leave to ferment for a day at room temperature. Whisk together the second preparation ingredients in the same way, add it to the first preparation and mix again. Cover with plastic wrap and let it ferment for another day. Whisk together the third preparation ingredients as for the others, add it to the levain and mix again. Cover with plastic wrap and let it ferment for half a day. Your levain is now ready to use.

THE DOUGH

In a bowl, dissolve the sugar in the water, then add the yeast, one portion of liquid levain and 125 g (4½ oz) flour. Whisk them together and let the mixture ferment for 2–3 minutes. Add the milk powder, butter, salt and another 125 g of the flour and mix well. Continue to add the flour and combine until you have a dough that holds together well and comes away from the bowl. Tip the dough onto your work surface and knead for about 8 minutes until it is quite smooth but not too stiff. Add a little flour if necessary. Scrape out your mixing bowl, then lightly oil it with a little vegetable oil and place the dough inside. Cover with plastic wrap and allow it to rise at room temperature for about 2 hours until it has doubled in size.

SHAPING THE DOUGH

When the dough has doubled in size, punch it down to release the air and turn it out onto a floured work surface. Let it rest for a few minutes, then divide it into two pieces. Roll out each piece to a thickness of 1.5 cm (⅝ inch) and cut out circles using a 9 cm (3½ inch) round cutter. Dust two or three baking trays with semolina flour and place the circles of dough on top. Scatter over some more semolina flour, cover with plastic wrap and allow them to rise for about 1 hour.

COOKING

Preheat the oven to 180°C (350°F/Gas 4). Heat a frying pan over medium heat and carefully transfer three or four muffins to the pan, depending on the size of your pan (don't add too many at once). Cook them for 5–10 minutes on each side until they have a good colour. Finish the cooking in the oven for another 5 minutes to make sure they are cooked right through.

tip: keep your levain in an airtight container in the refrigerator for 5–7 days. After that, you need to refresh it with equal quantities of hot water and flour. For example, 100 ml (3½ fl oz) hot water for 100 g (3½ oz/ ⅔ cup) strong flour. Take the levain out of the refrigerator, mix as above and let it ferment a little while before returning it to the refrigerator.

SUMO
BURGERS
ASK ME!
ZEPPOLES
VARIETY OF
DESSERTS

12 : 42

LUNCH TIME

BUNS FOR HAMBURGERS & HOT DOGS

For a great burger or a hot dog, the bun is at least as important as what you put in it. The real test for a bun is being good enough to eat by itself. These are.

MAKES 10 HAMBURGER BUNS OR 10 HOT DOG BUNS

Preparation time: 25 minutes
Resting time: about 2½ hours
Cooking time: 11–12 minutes

DRY INGREDIENTS

680 g (1 lb 8 oz) strong flour
2 teaspoons dried yeast
3 tablespoons caster (superfine) sugar
2 teaspoons salt

WET INGREDIENTS

145 ml (4¾ fl oz) water
50 g (1¾ oz) butter
185 ml (6 fl oz/¾ cup) milk
4 egg yolks

GLAZE

1½ tablespoons milk
sesame seeds (optional)

THE DOUGH

Combine all the dry ingredients. Heat the water and butter in a saucepan until the butter is melted. Remove from the heat and add the milk. Check the temperature of the mixture with a thermometer — it needs to be 49–55°C (120–130°F). Combine the two mixtures together. Start kneading and add the egg yolks one at a time, kneading well after each addition. Keep kneading until the dough is very elastic (10 minutes in an electric mixer, 10–20 minutes by hand). Form a smooth ball of dough, place it in an oiled container and cover with plastic wrap. Let it rise for about 1½ hours at room temperature until it has doubled in volume.

SHAPING AND THE SECOND RISE

Divide the dough into 10 equal portions.
For hamburger buns, shape the portions into balls between the palms of your hands and place them in round buttered and floured moulds, about 12 cm (4½ inches) in diameter and 2 cm (¾ inch) high.
For hot dog buns, form the balls into torpedo shapes — ideally, tubes about 12 cm long (4½ inches) and 4 cm (1½ inches) across — and put them in buttered and floured elongated moulds or a home-made equivalent made out of foil.
Place the moulds on a baking tray. Sprinkle with flour, then cover loosely with plastic wrap. Let them rise for at least 1 hour at room temperature until they have doubled in volume.

COOKING

Preheat the oven to 220°C (425°F/Gas 7). Glaze the buns by brushing them with the milk, but be careful not to crush them. Sprinkle with sesame seeds, if using. Cook the buns in the oven for 11–12 minutes until they're golden brown. The undersides should be lightly coloured.

CHEESEBURGER

It's easy to make a burger that's just okay. Taking your patties and hamburgers to the next level demands a little more effort, but it's really worth it. Here are the basic rules.

MAKES 2 CHEESEBURGERS

Preparation time: 15 minutes
Cooking time: 10 minutes

INGREDIENTS

200 g (7 oz) minced (ground)
    meat (see note)
2 slices cheese (cheddar, Comté …)
2 buns (page 102)
6 rounds pickled onion or
    other pickles (page 242)
lettuce and/or tomato
80 ml (2½ fl oz/⅓ cup) sauce
    (ketchup, mayonnaise,
    special sauce …)

SPECIAL SAUCE

120 g (4¼ oz/½ cup) mayonnaise
3 teaspoons ketchup
1 teaspoon mustard
1 teaspoon sweet pickles,
    finely chopped
1 teaspoon Tabasco® sauce
    (optional)

note: *the possible meat combinations are endless, you can even add pork, lamb, etc. What's key is that your minced meat should not be too lean — it should contain 15–25% fat. A popular New York combination is made up of half sirloin, a quarter blade and a quarter brisket. If you only use one cut, blade is probably your best choice.*

THE MEAT AND CHEESE

It's important to resist the temptation to press the meat into perfect compact pucks like the ready-made ones from the supermarket or the ones shaped by the butcher. Patties cook better when they are loosely put together, so you should work them with your hands and without pressing too hard. A good portion size is about 100 g (3½ oz), though it can be smaller. Brown the meat in a little butter or oil in a non-stick frying pan over medium–high heat, turning only once if possible. Gently press the meat with a spatula. After 3–5 minutes, when the first side is well browned, turn over the patty and cook the other side for 3–5 minutes. The temperature of the inside of the meat should be 60–70°C (140–160°F), according to taste. Check for doneness by pressing the patty with your fingers: the denser it feels, the more cooked it is. For a cheeseburger, add a slice or two of cheese on the browned side of the patty once it has been turned over. The cheese will melt while the meat continues to cook.

TOPPINGS AND BUNS

Make the toppings in advance. They might be lettuce, tomatoes, pickles (pickled onions, for example) and a sauce, such as ketchup (page 264), mayonnaise (page 264), or a special sauce, which is usually a mixture of different condiments.
Slice the buns in half and toast them just before starting to cook the meat so they are still warm when you serve the burger. You can toast them in a frying pan with a little butter, but this is optional.

ASSEMBLY

Spread the sauce on the bottom half of the toasted bun and put the cooked patty on top, followed by the other toppings such as lettuce or tomato. You can put sliced pickles under or on top of the meat.

THE PICKLED ONIONS

See 'fast pickles' recipe page 242.

FRENCH FRIES

See recipe page 128.

VEGGIE BURGER

A good vegetarian burger should be as fully satisfying for a meat eater as for a vegetarian. This is a patty recipe I've been fiddling with for years.

MAKES 4 PATTIES

Preparation time: 25 minutes
Cooking time: 45 minutes

TO COOK

100 g (3½ oz/½ cup) whole wheat
    or pearl barley (or a little more,
    given that volumes can vary)

TO SAUTÉ

3 teaspoons finely chopped onion
15 g (½ oz) mushrooms,
    thinly sliced
3 teaspoons cooking oil
2 pinches sweet or smoked
    paprika (optional)

OTHER INGREDIENTS

2 egg whites
175 g (6 oz) tinned red kidney
    beans, drained and rinsed
3 medjool dates, pitted
1 tablespoon cornflour (cornstarch)
2 tablespoons diced beetroot
    (beets), preferably raw
3 teaspoons soy sauce
2 pinches light brown sugar
2 tablespoons flat-leaf
    (Italian) parsley
1 teaspoon salt

COOKING THE WHEAT

The 100 g (3½ oz) of wheat plus three times its volume in water should give you 300 g (10½ oz) of cooked wheat, but to be safe you could cook a little more. Boil the water with the wheat, then lower the heat and simmer for about 30 minutes. If, when the water is absorbed, the wheat is still too hard, add more water and keep cooking until the wheat is as tender as you like it. If, on the other hand, the wheat is tender before all the water is absorbed, turn off the heat and drain off the excess water. Cool.

SAUTÉING THE VEGETABLES

Sauté the onions and mushrooms in the oil for about 5 minutes until the onions are translucent. Add the paprika to finish.

THE PATTIES

Process the sautéed vegetables and the cooked wheat with the other ingredients in a food processor, then, using slightly wet hands, shape the mixture into 4 patties.
In a frying pan, cook the patties in some oil over low heat, 5–7 minutes on each side until nicely browned, then turn them over carefully with a wide, thin spatula. For uniformly shaped patties, use a round cutter filled to three-quarters in the frying pan. Remove it before turning over the patty.

THE BURGER

Serve on buns with sauce and toppings as for meat hamburgers (page 104).

SWEET POTATOES

See 'home fries' recipe page 265.

EGGPLANT BURGER

This is a hybrid of two of my favourite New York sandwiches:
the diner 'pizza burger' and the traditional Italian 'eggplant parmesan sub'.

SERVES 2

Preparation time: 20 minutes
Resting time: 30 minutes
Cooking time: 20 minutes

PATTIES

1 eggplant (aubergine)
2 teaspoons salt
150 g (5½ oz/1 cup) plain
   (all-purpose) flour
1 egg
1 teaspoon milk
150 g (5½ oz/1⅓ cups)
   dry breadcrumbs
1 teaspoon dried oregano
1 teaspoon dried basil
100 ml (3½ fl oz) cooking oil
   (add more if needed)

OTHER INGREDIENTS

250 g (9 oz) fresh mozzarella
   cheese, sliced
25 g (1 oz) parmesan cheese, grated
250 ml (9 fl oz/1 cup) tomato
   sauce (page 166)
2 buns (page 102)

THE PATTIES

Cut the eggplant into slices about 1 cm (½ inch) thick.
Sprinkle with the salt and let them drain in a colander
for 30 minutes. Dry the slices on paper towels.
Have a bowl ready with the flour. In another bowl, beat the egg with the
milk. In a third bowl, combine the breadcrumbs and the dried herbs.
Heat about 2 cm (¾ inch) of oil in a fairly deep frying pan over medium
heat. Dip the slices of eggplant firstly in the flour, then in the egg and finally
in the breadcrumbs. Fry in the oil for a few minutes until golden on each
side and drain on paper towels. Preheat the oven to 210°C (415°F/Gas 6–7).

COOKING AND ASSEMBLY

On a baking tray lined with baking paper, put together four stacks
(one per half bun), alternating slices of eggplant and the two kinds
of cheese, sometimes putting a little tomato sauce under the cheese.
Bake for a few minutes until the cheese starts to bubble.
While the stacks are cooking, open the hamburger buns and toast
them in a little butter in a frying pan until lightly browned.
On a serving plate, cover the cut sides of the buns with
tomato sauce. Place the cooked eggplant stacks on top.
Insert a toothpick to hold the burgers together.

GREEK SALAD

See recipe page 112.

GREEK SALAD

In terms of Greek salad, the benchmark for me is the generous version served at Big Nick's joint on the Upper West Side of Manhattan, where it comes with a dressing full of crunch.

SERVES 4

Preparation time: 20 minutes
Refrigeration time: 30 minutes

DRESSING

55 ml (1¾ fl oz) olive oil
30 ml (1 fl oz) lemon juice
30 ml (1 fl oz) red wine vinegar
½ teaspoon dried oregano
2 garlic cloves, crushed
2 pinches salt + 1 turn of
    the pepper mill
3 teaspoons finely chopped red onion
3 teaspoons finely chopped
    capsicum (pepper), preferably
    yellow or orange

SALAD

250 g (9 oz) cherry or grape tomatoes
3 anchovies
1 small Lebanese (short)
    cucumber, seeded and diced
2 capsicums (peppers) preferably
    yellow or orange, diced
½ red onion, diced
250 g (9 oz) feta cheese, diced
100 g (3½ oz) black dry-salted olives

THE DRESSING

Whisk the oil, lemon juice, vinegar and oregano together, then add the remaining ingredients and combine.

THE SALAD

Cut the tomatoes in half lengthways. Halve the anchovies and put them, the cucumber, capsicum and onion in a salad bowl. Add the feta and black olives, pour over the dressing and mix gently so as not to crush the feta and anchovies. Refrigerate for at least 30 minutes and serve cold.

DILL POTATO SALAD

This salad is the perfect side for your meat sandwiches.

SERVES 6

Preparation time: 20 minutes
Cooking time: 10 minutes
Refrigeration time: 1 hour

SALAD

700 g (1 lb 9 oz) new potatoes
50 g (1¾ oz) red onion,
    finely chopped
1½ tablespoons capers

DRESSING

40 g (1½ oz) caster (superfine) sugar
2 pinches salt + 2 turns
    of the pepper mill
1 garlic clove, chopped
1½ tablespoons rice vinegar
60 g (2¼ oz/¼ cup) plain
    mayonnaise (page 264)
60 g (2¼ oz/¼ cup) natural yoghurt
1 tablespoon dill, finely chopped

THE SALAD

Peel and cut the potatoes into quarters or smaller if the potatoes
are large. Place in a saucepan of cold water. Bring the water and
potatoes to the boil and cook for about 10 minutes over medium
heat. Test for doneness with a knife: the potato cubes should
still be just a little firm. Drain and rinse with cold water.
Put the red onion in a bowl of cold water for a few minutes, then drain
carefully. Place the cooled potato, red onion and capers in a salad bowl.

THE DRESSING

Combine all of the ingredients except the dill in a large bowl.

SERVING

Combine the dressing with the mixture of potatoes and
red onion. Add the dill and stir the salad gently so as not
to crush the potatoes. Refrigerate and serve chilled.

MACARONI SALAD

The tiny pieces of raw vegetables make all the difference.

SERVES 5

Preparation time: 20 minutes
Cooking time: 10 minutes
Refrigeration time: 30 minutes

SALAD

250 g (9 oz) macaroni
olive oil
300 g (10½ oz) carrot
70 g (2½ oz) celery
12 small pickles, chopped

DRESSING

300 g (10½ oz) plain mayonnaise (page 264)
55 ml (1¾ fl oz) rice vinegar (preferably
   flavoured with tarragon)
1 tablespoon caster (superfine) sugar
2 pinches salt + 2 turns of the pepper mill
1½ tablespoons flat-leaf (Italian)
   parsley, finely chopped

THE SALAD

Cook the pasta until *al dente* in a large saucepan of salted water. Drain and rinse under cold water. Drizzle with olive oil so the macaroni doesn't stick together. Peel the carrots, trim the base and leaves of the celery stalks and finely chop both. Gently combine the carrots, celery, pickles and macaroni in a salad bowl.

THE DRESSING

Whisk the dressing ingredients together, then gently mix into the macaroni. Refrigerate for at least 30 minutes before serving.

DILL POTATO SALAD AND COLESLAW

See recipes page 114 and page 265.

WALDORF SALAD

*This salad of apple and celery, now a classic,
was created in the late 1890s by Oscar Tschirky,
the maître d'hôtel at the Waldorf Astoria in New York.*

SERVES 1

Preparation time: 30 minutes
Cooking time: 10 minutes

SALAD

60 ml (2 fl oz/¼ cup) water
55 g (2 oz/¼ cup) caster
    (superfine) sugar
125 g (4½ oz/1¼ cups) pecans
200 g (7 oz) celeriac
2 granny smith apples (about
    300 g/10½ oz), cored, not peeled

DRESSING

80 g (2¾ oz) lemon
    mayonnaise (page 264)
95 g (3¼ oz/⅓ cup) natural yoghurt
1 teaspoon honey
1 pinch salt + 1 turn of
    the pepper mill
2 teaspoons snipped chives

THE SALAD

Place the water, sugar and whole pecans in a saucepan,
bring to a simmer over medium heat and cook for about
8–10 minutes. The syrup takes on a light colour and when the
pecans are well coated, empty the contents of the saucepan
onto a wire rack placed over a tray. Separate the pecans with
a spatula so you don't burn yourself. Allow to cool.
Cut the celeriac and apples into matchsticks using a knife
or a food processor. Place them in a bowl of cold water.

THE DRESSING

Combine all of the ingredients except the chives in a salad bowl.

ASSEMBLING AND SERVING

Drain the celeriac and apples and dry them well with paper
towels or a clean tea towel (dish towel). Combine them
with the dressing. Add the chives and refrigerate.
At serving time, add the caramelised pecans.

CAESAR SALAD

A lot of restaurants used to make a big show of preparing this salad in front of customers at the table. Today, table-prepared Caesar salads are rare, but a fresh home-made dressing is still a must.

SERVES 1

Preparation time: 20 minutes

DRESSING

1 egg yolk
3 teaspoons lemon juice
1 teaspoon dijon mustard
90 ml (3 fl oz) sunflower or canola oil
1 teaspoon anchovy paste (or the same amount of crushed anchovies) or Worcestershire sauce
½ teaspoon acacia or other light honey
3 garlic cloves, crushed
2 tablespoons grated parmesan cheese, plus extra to serve

SALAD

12 leaves of cos (romaine) lettuce
6 large croutons (page 264)
3 teaspoons capers

THE DRESSING

All of the ingredients should be at room temperature to facilitate the emulsion. In a deep bowl, whisk the egg yolk, lemon juice and mustard until well blended. Pour in the oil very slowly while continuing to whisk. Once you have a nice emulsion, add the rest of the dressing ingredients and mix until combined.

THE SALAD

Wash, dry and cut the lettuce. Gently combine the lettuce with the dressing then transfer the dressed lettuce to a serving platter or bowl. Top with the croutons, capers and extra parmesan.

tip: *make your own anchovy paste by crushing whole anchovies with a fork. Process them with the sauce until perfectly smooth.*

BLT (BACON, LETTUCE & TOMATO)

This simple bacon sandwich can be as great or mediocre as the ingredients you choose to use. Putting it together is utterly simple.

MAKES 1 SANDWICH

Preparation time: 10 minutes
Cooking time: 10 minutes

INGREDIENTS

3 or 4 slices of smoked bacon
2 slices bread
1 tablespoon unsalted butter
1½ tablespoons mayonnaise
(page 264)
2 or 3 lettuce leaves
2 or 3 slices of tomato

THE BREAD

Brown the bacon in a frying pan (see page 88). While the bacon is cooking, toast and butter the slices of bread, then spread them with mayonnaise. Season with salt and pepper.

THE FILLING

Stack the lettuce, tomato and bacon on one of the two bread slices and top the sandwich with the other slice.
You can poke a toothpick into the sandwich to help it hold together better, then cut it in half.

tip: timing is important. Ideally, you want the toast and bacon to still be warm when you serve the sandwich. A BLT that has been sitting around should still be enjoyable to eat, but not quite as over-the-top as a fresh hot one.

GRILLED CHEESE SANDWICH

With such a simple dish as a grilled cheese sandwich, having high-quality ingredients will obviously be key.

MAKES 1 SANDWICH

Preparation time: 5 minutes
Cooking time: about 5 minutes

INGREDIENTS

2 slices sandwich bread
50–70 g (1¾–2½ oz) cheese slices
    (cheddar is the most traditional
    choice, but any good cheese,
    such as Comté, Cantal or
    emmental, will work well)
30 g (1 oz) unsalted butter, softened

Heat a frying pan over medium–low heat. Generously smear half the butter on one side of one of the slices of bread and place the slice, buttered side down, in the frying pan. Lay the sliced cheese on top. Generously butter the other slice of bread and place it on top of the cheese slice in the pan, buttered side up.

After a couple of minutes, when the bottom slice is nicely browned, slide a wide spatula underneath and, holding the sandwich together with your free hand, turn it over. Continue cooking until the second side is golden brown and the cheese starts oozing out the sides. If your bread is looking browned before the cheese starts to ooze, the heat is too high.

note: *there are endless variations on the basic grilled cheese sandwich. In addition to mixing up different types of bread and cheese, some common additions to the sandwich include mayonnaise, ham, tomato and tuna salad. With tuna salad, it's called a 'tuna melt' (see recipe page 126).*

TUNA MELT

A grilled cheese sandwich with a tuna salad filling.
This is my tuna salad recipe.

MAKES 2 CLUB SANDWICHES
Preparation time: 15 minutes
Cooking time: 10–12 minutes

TUNA SALAD
200 g (7 oz) tinned tuna (drained)
2 tablespoons olive oil
2 teaspoons lemon juice
3 teaspoons acacia or
    other light honey
2 teaspoons dijon mustard
70 g (2½ oz) celery, finely chopped
1 tablespoon finely chopped onion
60 g (2¼ oz/¼ cup) mayonnaise
salt and pepper

SANDWICHES
70 g (2½ oz) unsalted butter
6 slices sandwich bread
8 cheese slices

THE TUNA SALAD
Mix all of the ingredients together with a fork until well combined. Drain the salad in a large colander to remove excess liquid.

ASSEMBLY
Butter the slices of bread. Pan-fry one of the slices, buttered side down, with a slice of cheese on top. Set the slice aside: this will be the middle slice of the sandwich.
On a second slice of bread, place another slice of cheese on the unbuttered side, then some tuna salad and more cheese. Top with the already browned slice, then add some tuna salad, a slice of cheese and the last slice of bread, buttered side out.
Pan-fry the sandwich for 3–4 minutes on each side over very low heat. Cut the sandwich on the diagonal, then proceed in the same way for the second sandwich.

FRENCH FRIES
See recipe page 128.

FRENCH FRIES

The two stages of deep-frying are the key to making perfect fries.

SERVES 6

Preparation time: 10 minutes
Resting time: 1 hour
Cooking time: 5 minutes

INGREDIENTS

1 kg (2 lb 4 oz) sebago or
    coliban potatoes (allow about
    120 g/4¼ oz per serve)
oil suitable for frying,
such as grapeseed oil

CUTTING

Peel the potatoes using a mandolin, knife or another tool of
your choice, then cut into long and uniform pieces.
Soak them in cold water for 1 hour to remove the surface
starch, which will stop the fries from darkening too much
during cooking. Drain and pat the potatoes dry.

FRYING

In a deep-fryer or large saucepan, heat the oil until it reaches 160°C
(315°F). Fry the potatoes for 2–3 minutes until they start to bend but
are still quite pale. Drain and allow to cool at room temperature.
Increase the temperature of the oil to 190°C (375°F) and fry the
potatoes again for 2–3 more minutes until they're nicely browned.
Undercooked fries will be too soft, because not enough water has
evaporated. Overcooked fries will be too greasy because they will
have absorbed too much oil. Perfectly cooked fries take practice.

SERVING

Drain the fries on paper towels. If you're not serving them immediately,
or if you're cooking them in batches, keep them warm in a preheated
100°C (200°F/Gas ½) oven. Season with salt before serving.

LATKES

*Crispy on the outside, soft in the middle, these Ashkenazi potato pancakes
are yet another delicious addition to New York's glorious tradition of fried potato.*

MAKES 12 LATKES

Preparation time: 20 minutes
Cooking time: 40 minutes

INGREDIENTS

1 kg (2 lb 4 oz) sebago or
    coliban potatoes
1½ tablespoons salt
cooking oil (enough for
a depth of 1.5 cm/⅝ inch
    in the cooking pan)
1 large brown onion, finely chopped
3 eggs, lightly whisked
50 g (1¾ oz) matzo meal or potato
    starch (extra if necessary)
apple sauce and/or sour
cream, to serve

THE POTATOES

Peel and grate half the potatoes (500 g/1 lb 2 oz), mix in the salt, cover
with cold water and set aside while you prepare the boiled potatoes.
Peel the other half of the potatoes and cut them into small pieces. Place
them in a saucepan of cold water. Bring to the boil, then lower the heat
to a simmer and cook for about 15 minutes until the potatoes are tender.
Drain them, allow to cool and mash them with a fork or potato masher.

COOKING THE LATKES

Heat the oil in a deep frying pan over medium heat. Squeeze as much
water as possible out of the grated potatoes and add them to the mashed
potatoes along with the onion and eggs. Add the matzo meal or potato
starch to thicken the mixture so that the patties aren't overly wet when you
put them in the oil. Test the oil with a little potato mixture — it should
be just hot enough to sizzle, but not so hot that it burns straight away.
Shape the mixture into 12 patties between the palms of your hands and place
half of them in the oil. After a minute of frying, flatten the patties a little with
the back of a spatula. After about 5 minutes, turn them over and continue
cooking on the other side for another 5 minutes or so. If the underside of
the latkes is cooking too slowly or too quickly, adjust the heat accordingly.
Season with salt and pepper and repeat with the remaining patties.

SERVING

Drain the latkes on paper towels. If you're not serving them immediately,
or if you're cooking them in batches, keep the latkes warm in a preheated
100°C (200°F/Gas ½) oven. Serve with apple sauce and/or sour cream.

note: *feel free to replace the potatoes with other root
vegetables such as sweet potato or celeriac.*

PIEROGI

*Pierogi, sautéed potato ravioli, are one of the things
I love to eat in Polish or Ukrainian restaurants, such as the
Stage Restaurant in Manhattan's Lower East Side.*

MAKES 25 PIEROGI

Preparation time: 1 hour
Resting time: 1 hour
Cooking time: 50–55 minutes

PASTA DOUGH (FOR 50 PIEROGI)

500 g (1 lb 2 oz/3⅓ cups)
   plain (all-purpose) flour
1 teaspoon salt
3 teaspoons sunflower oil
1 egg
250 ml (9 fl oz/1 cup) water

FILLING (FOR 25 PIEROGI)

375 g (13 oz) potatoes
1 brown onion, finely chopped
1½ tablespoons cooking oil

TOPPING

2 brown onions, roughly chopped
60 ml (2 fl oz/¼ cup) cooking oil
sour cream or apple sauce, to serve

THE PASTA DOUGH

Process all of the ingredients together and knead until the dough is very elastic (5–10 minutes in an electric mixer, 10–20 minutes by hand). Form a smooth ball of dough. Place the dough in an oiled container, cover with plastic wrap and let it rest for 1 hour at room temperature. Divide into two portions so that each is large enough to make 25 pierogi. The unused portion of dough can be wrapped in plastic wrap and frozen.

THE FILLING

Peel and cut the potatoes into small pieces of about the same size. Place in a saucepan of cold water. Bring to the boil, then lower the heat and simmer for about 15 minutes until the potatoes are tender. Drain. Meanwhile, sauté the chopped onion in the oil over medium heat for 5–10 minutes until softened and slightly brown. Mash the potatoes and onion into the oil with a fork. Season with salt and pepper.

SHAPING AND COOKING

Divide a portion of dough into 25 balls and roll them out into rounds 3 mm (⅛ inch) thick. Shape balls of filling using a tablespoon and place each ball on a round of pasta. Fold the pasta dough over and press the edges with a fork to seal well (see illustration). Cook the pierogi in a large saucepan of boiling water for about 5 minutes. Pour a little oil into the water and stir to stop the pierogi sticking together. Drain, then fry the pierogi in about 1 cm (½ inch) of butter or cooking oil until they are crisp and golden brown on all sides.

THE TOPPING

Sauté the onions in the oil over low heat, stirring occasionally, for about 20 minutes until they are translucent. Continue cooking over medium heat, continuing to stir, for another 5–10 minutes until they're well browned but not burnt. Scatter them over the hot sautéed pierogi and serve with sour cream or apple sauce on the side.

CHINATOWN

A neighbourhood that expresses a world of its own: traditional Chinese restaurants serving Sichuan and Cantonese food, Vietnamese and Malaysian restaurants, Peking duck restaurants, fish markets, coffee shops, yum cha, bubble tea cafés, ice cream shops and more …

RESTAURANT 34

34 沾記酒家

PORK BUNS

In a typical New York mixed marriage, this popular Chinatown fast food can be recreated at home by combining the basic challah dough recipe with a not-particularly-kosher pork shoulder, marinated in a home-made char siu sauce with no MSG or food colouring.

MAKES 15 BUNS

Preparation time: 15 minutes
Marinating time: 12–24 hours
Cooking time: 1–1 hour 15 minutes
Resting time: 1 hour

CHAR SIU MARINADE

30 g (1 oz) peanut butter (page 263)
125 ml (4 fl oz/½ cup) soy sauce
225 g (8 oz) acacia or other light
  honey or liquid glucose
2 garlic cloves, crushed
2 teaspoons rice vinegar
45 ml (1½ fl oz) rice vinegar
  or Mei Kuei Lu Chiew
  (Chinese rose wine)
1½ teaspoons Chinese five-spice
2 pinches bicarbonate of
  soda (baking soda)

INGREDIENTS

750 g (1 lb 10 oz) pork
  shoulder or loin
2 pinches cornflour (cornstarch)
1 quantity challah dough (page 14)

THE MARINADE

In a bowl, make a slurry by combining the peanut butter with the same amount of soy sauce. Gradually add the rest of the soy sauce. Mix in the rest of the char siu marinade ingredients, finishing with the bicarbonate of soda. For a saucier bun, set aside 2–3 tablespoons of sauce before adding the bicarbonate of soda. You can dress the pork with this sauce after it has been baked and chopped, and before it is wrapped in the dough.

THE MEAT

Trim any excess fat from the pork and make a series of deep incisions at 2 cm (¾ inch) intervals. Cover the pork with the marinade inside a ziplock bag. Close the bag, removing as much air as possible, and place it in the refrigerator. The pork should be completely submerged in the sauce. Marinate for 12–24 hours. Preheat the oven to 230°C (450°F/Gas 8). Cook on a wire rack in a roasting pan for 45–55 minutes until the internal temperature reaches a minimum of 62°C (144°F). Allow the meat to cool and chop into small pieces. Toss the meat in the cornflour, then, if you put aside any char siu sauce without the bicarbonate of soda, add it to the meat as well.

SHAPING AND COOKING

Make the challah dough following the recipe on page 14 to the first rise. Divide the dough into 15 equal portions. Make a hollow in the middle of each portion of dough, place about 40 g (1½ oz) roast pork into the hollow and pinch the dough closed around the meat.
Place the closed buns on a baking tray lined with baking paper. Dust with flour and cover loosely with plastic wrap. Let the buns rise for 1 hour at room temperature.
Preheat the oven to 180°C (350°F/Gas 4). Brush the tops of the buns with the egg white and sugar glaze from the challah recipe. Cook the buns for 15–20 minutes until golden brown.

SESAME NOODLES

When I was a kid I always ordered these sweet and tangy noodles from the local Chinese take-out.

SERVES 3

Preparation time: 20 minutes
Cooking time: varies depending on the type of noodles

INGREDIENTS

800 g (1 lb 12 oz) fresh Chinese
    egg noodles (or 400 g/14 oz
    if they are dried)
100 g (3½ oz) sliced Lebanese
    (short) cucumbers or
    pickles, to serve
1–2 tablespoons toasted black or
    white sesame seeds, to serve

SAUCE

4 garlic cloves
1 tablespoon peeled and finely
    chopped fresh ginger
1–2 tablespoons sugar
    (according to taste)
135 ml (4½ fl oz) water
50 g (1¾ oz) Chinese sesame paste
55 ml (1¾ fl oz) sesame oil
50 g (1¾ oz) peanut
    butter (page 263)
1 tablespoon rice vinegar
1½ tablespoons soy sauce

THE NOODLES

Cook the noodles according to the packet directions.
Once cooked, drain and plunge into iced water.

THE SAUCE

Crush the garlic with a garlic press or chop it finely using a knife. Both garlic and ginger can then be ground in a mortar and pestle with the sugar or blended with the water in a blender or food processor. The aim is to grind up the garlic and ginger as finely as possible.

Mix in the rest of the sauce ingredients and whisk with a whisk or fork until well combined.

Pour the sauce over the noodles gradually until they're as saucy as you like them, tossing them gently with fingers or a chopstick to avoid crushing them.

SERVING

Serve cold with slices of cucumber or pickle and a sprinkling of toasted sesame seeds.

SPICED PINEAPPLE

See 'fast pickles' recipes page 242.

tip: if you have raw sesame seeds, you can spread them out in one layer in a frying pan over medium heat and toast them, shaking the pan from time to time, for about 3 minutes until they're evenly browned.

BAXTER STREET

*My colleague Ngan Tran, who grew up in Vietnamese restaurants
in the south of France, was kind enough to share her family's
recipes for two favourite dishes I used to eat in Chinatown.*

CLAYPOT SALMON
SERVES 4

Preparation time: 15 minutes
Resting time: 2 hours to overnight
Cooking time: 25 minutes

INGREDIENTS

4 salmon steaks
90 ml (3 fl oz) fish sauce
45 ml (1½ fl oz) mushroom
dark soy sauce
1½ tablespoons sugar
2 garlic cloves, crushed
4 large pieces of fresh pineapple
coriander (cilantro) leaves, to serve

GREEN PAPAYA SALAD
SERVES 4

Preparation time: 15 minutes
Cooking time: 5 minutes

INGREDIENTS

1 green papaya, peeled and shredded
2 carrots, shredded
½ bunch mint, coarsely chopped
½ bunch coriander (cilantro),
coarsely chopped
45 ml (1½ fl oz) sunflower oil
2 garlic cloves, chopped
1½ limes, juiced
80 ml (2½ fl oz/⅓ cup) fish sauce
3 teaspoons grated palm
sugar (jaggery)
1 teaspoon salt
1 chilli, chopped (optional)
fresh ginger, chopped, to taste
2 tablespoons toasted
peanuts, chopped

CLAYPOT SALMON

THE MARINADE

Make the marinade the night before, or at least 2 hours before
cooking. Place the steaks in a mixing bowl and pour over 3
tablespoons fish sauce, 1 tablespoon mushroom dark soy sauce,
half the sugar and 1 crushed garlic clove. Combine gently, cover
with plastic wrap and set aside. Refrigerate if resting overnight.

COOKING

Drizzle some oil in a flameproof casserole dish or heavy saucepan
and lay the drained salmon steaks, pineapple and the remaining
crushed garlic clove on top. Add the remaining fish sauce, mushroom
dark soy sauce, sugar and some salt. Cover with water and bring to
the boil. Adjust the seasoning (the sauce should be both sweet and
salty), then carefully turn the steaks over. Cook at a gentle simmer
on a low heat, covered, for 20–25 minutes. The sauce should reduce
to just a caramelised layer in the bottom of the pan; if this is not
the case, uncover and continue to reduce for a few minutes.

SERVING

Garnish with coriander, season generously with pepper and serve with
white rice and a salad or soup.

GREEN PAPAYA SALAD

THE SALAD

Combine the green papaya, carrots, mint and coriander.

THE DRESSING

In a small saucepan, heat the oil over low heat and fry the chopped
garlic. Once browned, allow to cool in the oil. Make the sauce by
combining the lime juice, fish sauce, palm sugar, salt and chopped
chilli. Add the toasted garlic and oil, and the ginger. Pour the
dressing over the salad just before serving. Gently toss and sprinkle
with the peanuts.

ROAST CHICKEN

To achieve a roast chicken at home with skin as crispy and meat as flavourful as the ones from the rotisseries on Manhattan's Upper West Side, I employ two techniques: I marinate the chicken in a salt-water brine; and I cook it slowly on a rack.

FOR A 1.5–2 KG (3 LB 5 OZ–4 LB 8 OZ) CHICKEN

Preparation time: 15 minutes
Resting time: at least 5 hours
Cooking time: 2½–3 hours

BRINE

3.6 litres (126 fl oz) water
500 g (1 lb 2 oz) non-iodised salt
300 g (10½ oz) sugar
2 teaspoons black or yellow
    mustard seeds
1 teaspoon black peppercorns
2 lemons, quartered

RUB

60 g (2¼ oz/¼ cup)
butter or olive oil
2 tablespoons acacia or other light
    honey or maple syrup (optional)
1–2 teaspoons cayenne pepper
1–2 teaspoons ground cumin
2 teaspoons salt
3 pinches ground black pepper

BRINING AND DRYING

Combine all of the brining ingredients together, except for the quartered lemons, in a large pot and stir over high heat until the sugar and salt have dissolved. Allow to cool at room temperature. As it takes a while for the brine to cool down, do this the day before or replace 500 ml (17 fl oz/2 cups) water with ice, which you can add once everything is dissolved, to quickly lower the temperature. In a large pot or bucket, submerge the chicken in the cooled brine with the quartered lemons. Cover and refrigerate for at least 2 hours per kilogram (2 lb 4 oz), but not for more than 12 hours. Rinse, pat dry with paper towels and let it rest again in the refrigerator on a wire rack, uncovered, for 2–12 hours — air-drying the chicken in this way will help make the chicken more crispy.

RUBBING AND COOKING

Preheat the oven to 120°C (235°F/Gas ½). Whisk all of the rub ingredients together and spread over the whole of the chicken and inside the cavity. Place the chicken on its back on a V-shaped roasting rack (see photo). Cook for 1½ hours. Turn the chicken over and return to the oven for another 1–1½ hours until the juices run clear when you pierce the chicken with a knife or skewer, or until a meat thermometer inserted into the deepest part of the thigh reads at least 75°C (165°F).

MATZO BALL SOUP

The matzo balls are really the star attraction in this soup, but you can make it without them, in which case it would just be a classic chicken soup (aka 'Jewish penicillin').

SERVES 5

Preparation time: 30 minutes
Refrigeration time: 3 hours
Cooking time: 45 minutes

BALLS

150 g (5½ oz) matzo meal
2 pinches bicarbonate of
    soda (baking soda)
1 teaspoon ground
    cinnamon (optional)
4 eggs, separated
60 ml (2 fl oz/¼ cup) olive oil
60 ml (2 fl oz/¼ cup) water
1 teaspoon parsley, finely chopped
½ teaspoon salt

BASE

1 carrot, diced
1 parsnip, diced
1 brown onion, finely chopped
4 garlic cloves, crushed
1 teaspoon dried thyme
2 tablespoons olive oil
2 litres (70 fl oz/8 cups)
    chicken stock (page 265)
100 g (3½ oz) dried egg noodles
12 small pieces of cooked
    chicken (e.g. chicken leftovers,
    see previous page)

THE BALLS

Mix together the matzo meal, bicarbonate of soda and cinnamon. Beat together the egg yolks, oil, water and parsley. Combine the two mixtures.

Beat the egg whites with the salt until stiff peaks form. Gently fold the beaten egg whites into the rest and refrigerate for at least 3 hours. With oiled hands, roll the matzo ball dough into balls the size of a ping-pong ball.

THE BASE

Sauté the vegetables, garlic and thyme in the olive oil over medium heat for about 5 minutes until the onion is translucent, then add the chicken stock. Bring to the boil, then lower the heat to a simmer. Season with salt and pepper. Add the matzo balls 30 minutes before serving, the dried egg noodles 10 minutes before serving and the pieces of chicken 5 minutes before serving. To reduce the total cooking time, the matzo balls can also be pre-cooked separately in salted water and then added to the soup with the chicken just before serving.

MUSHROOM BARLEY SOUP

Super tender slow-cooked beef cheek is the key to this rustic winter classic.

SERVES 8

Preparation time: 30 minutes
Cooking time: about 4 hours

STOCK AND MEAT

1 onion, roughly chopped
1½ tablespoons olive oil
50 g (1¾ oz) celery,
    roughly chopped
50 g (1¾ oz) carrot,
    roughly chopped
250 g (9 oz) beef cheeks,
    cut into large cubes
4 garlic cloves
100 ml (3½ fl oz) white wine
2 teaspoons salt
3 litres (105 fl oz/12 cups) water

OTHER INGREDIENTS

150 g (5½ oz) whole barley or wheat
500 g (1 lb 2 oz) mushrooms,
    thinly sliced
45 ml (1½ fl oz) olive oil
1 onion, chopped
200 g (7 oz) combination of celery,
    carrot and parsnip, diced
2 bay leaves
1 large sprig thyme
45 ml (1½ fl oz) white wine
25 g (1 oz) cornflour
    (cornstarch) (adjust according
    to the consistency)
parsley, to serve

THE STOCK AND THE MEAT

In a soup pot, sauté the onion in the olive oil over medium heat until translucent. Add the celery and carrot and cook for another 5 minutes. Add the beef cheek and continue cooking for 5 minutes, stirring until browned on all sides. Add the garlic and continue to cook for a couple of minutes. Add the white wine and cook for a few minutes, then add the salt and water. Bring to the boil, then reduce the heat and simmer over low heat for 2½ hours, skimming and discarding any scum that rises to the surface.

Remove the meat and set aside to add back to the soup later. Strain the rest through a colander over a bowl or large saucepan and discard the solids. You should have a little more than 2 litres (70 fl oz/8 cups) of stock, which you can set aside. If the stock has reduced to less than this, you can extend it by adding more water.

THE SOUP

Rinse the barley or wheat and cook in boiling water (at least three times the volume of the barley) for about 30 minutes until tender. Drain the barley and set aside.

Cut the meat into small pieces and set aside. It should be super tender at this point and will more or less disintegrate into small strands when it goes back into the soup.

In a soup pot, sauté the mushrooms in the olive oil over high heat for a few minutes, then add the onion, celery, carrot, parsnip, bay leaves and thyme and lower the heat to medium. Cook for a further 5 minutes, stirring. Add the reserved stock, bring to the boil, then lower the heat to a simmer. Cook for about 20 minutes or until the vegetables are tender. Blend the white wine with the cornflour, mix it into the soup and simmer until slightly thickened. Season with salt and pepper.

SERVING

Add the meat and barley to the simmering soup 5 minutes before serving. Serve garnished with some chopped parsley.

SPLIT PEA SOUP

On a cold winter's day, a hot bowl of smooth split pea soup with a few croutons thrown in hits the spot like nothing else.

SERVES 5

Preparation time: 30 minutes
Soaking time: overnight
Cooking time: 1 hour 45 minutes

INGREDIENTS

500 g (1 lb 2 oz) split green peas
60 ml (2 fl oz/¼ cup) olive oil
1 onion, roughly chopped
100 g (3½ oz) carrots,
    roughly chopped
50 g (1¾ oz) celery,
    roughly chopped
3 garlic cloves, chopped
1 teaspoon smoked paprika
1 teaspoon ground cumin
1 bunch coriander (cilantro),
    stems and leaves separated
1.5 litres (52 fl oz/6 cups) water
2 teaspoons cider vinegar
3 teaspoons sugar
1 teaspoon salt
½ teaspoon ground black pepper

GARNISH

95 g (3¼ oz/⅓ cup) yoghurt
    or sour cream (optional)
about 20 croutons (page 264)

THE SPLIT PEAS

Soak the split peas in cold water overnight. Discard the water and rinse. While many recipes indicate that it is not necessary to soak split peas, I find that pre-soaking them produces a less starchy, more digestible soup that is also easier to make since it cooks faster and doesn't stick as much to the saucepan. You could, however, skip this step, but you should at least rinse the split peas.

COOKING

Heat 1½ tablespoons of the olive oil in a soup pot over medium heat. Sauté the onion, carrot, celery and garlic and cook for about 5 minutes. Add the spices and chopped coriander stems and cook for another 5 minutes, stirring regularly.

Add the rinsed peas and cover them with about three-quarters of the water. Bring to the boil and then lower the heat. Simmer for 1½ hours or more, until the peas are soft and naturally disintegrate into a purée. Skim and discard any scum that rises to the top as you go. Check regularly that the peas are not sticking to the bottom of the pot; if they start to catch, turn off the heat. After a few minutes, the stuck (but hopefully not burnt) layer should come away easily with a spatula and you can then resume simmering the soup.

Blend the soup with a hand blender until smooth. Add as much of the remaining water as needed, and more if necessary, to achieve the desired consistency. Add the vinegar, remaining oil, sugar, salt and pepper.

THE GARNISH

Ladle the soup into bowls. Finely chop the coriander leaves, then scatter over the soup. Drop 1 tablespoon of yoghurt or sour cream in each bowl, then add a few croutons.

CORN BREAD

See recipe page 150.

CORN BREAD

This cake–bread from the American south is usually enjoyed with savoury food,
but it is also delicious on its own with a little butter and jam or honey.

MAKES 16 PIECES

Preparation time: 10 minutes
Cooking time: about 45 minutes

DRY INGREDIENTS

200 g (7 oz/1⅓ cups) plain
    (all-purpose) flour
200 g (7 oz) fine polenta (cornmeal)
1½ teaspoons baking powder
2 pinches bicarbonate of
    soda (baking soda)
½ teaspoon salt

WET INGREDIENTS

400 ml (14 fl oz) buttermilk
70 g (2½ oz) unsalted butter, melted
2 eggs
175 g (6 oz) cooked corn
    kernels off the cob
⅓ small green chilli, finely
    chopped (optional)

THE BATTER

Preheat the oven to 190°C (375°F/Gas 5). Butter a square 24 cm (9½ inch)
cake tin and sprinkle with sugar.
Combine all the dry ingredients together, then beat together the wet
ingredients. Combine the two mixtures without overworking the batter.

COOKING

Pour the batter into the tin and bake for about 45 minutes
until a skewer inserted into the middle comes out clean.

MAC & CHEESE

Feed the kids (or your inner child). Nobody in any case is ever disappointed with this gratin of macaroni with a cheese sauce.

SERVES 5

Preparation time: 20 minutes
Cooking time: about 50 minutes

INGREDIENTS

500 g (1 lb 2 oz) macaroni

CHEESE SAUCE

50 g (1¾ oz) butter
1½ tablespoons plain (all-purpose) flour
400 ml (14 fl oz) evaporated milk
1 teaspoon dijon mustard
2 teaspoons salt
300 ml (10½ fl oz) milk
300 g (10½ oz/3 cups) grated cheddar cheese (or similar cheese, such as gouda or Cantal)

GRATIN

150 g (5½ oz) day old breadcrumbs
50 g (1¾ oz) unsalted butter, melted

THE PASTA

Cook the macaroni pasta in salted water according to the packet directions until *al dente*. Drain and rinse with cold water to stop it cooking further.

THE CHEESE SAUCE

Heat the butter in a saucepan over medium heat. After a few minutes, when bubbles start to form, add the flour. Stir constantly while cooking the mixture until it starts to turn a light brown. Add the evaporated milk slowly while continuing to stir. Mix in the mustard and salt. Continue stirring and cooking for another few minutes until smooth and thick. Add the milk and cheese and stir until the cheese is melted. Turn off the heat and add the cooked macaroni to the sauce.

THE GRATIN

Preheat the oven to 180°C (350°F/Gas 4). Transfer the macaroni and cheese to an appropriately sized baking dish. It's normal for the mixture to seem quite liquid, but it will thicken during cooking. Combine the breadcrumbs and melted butter and sprinkle over the top. Bake for 30 minutes.

tip: for a cheesier version, reduce the quantity of pasta by 20–25%.

NOODLE KUGLE

See recipe page 154.

NOODLE KUGLE

In my family, we like to have warm noodle pudding with roast chicken, but it is also great cold on its own the next day.

SERVES 10

Preparation time: 20 minutes
Cooking time: about 1 hour

BASE

250 g (9 oz) dried egg noodles
6 eggs, beaten
45 ml (1½ fl oz) sunflower oil
325 g (11½ oz) rhubarb compote
100 g (3½ oz) light brown
    sugar (or 95 g/3¼ oz sugar
    + 1 teaspoon molasses)
70 g (2½ oz) raisins
3 teaspoons ground cinnamon
½ teaspoon salt

TOPPING

150 g (5½ oz) granny
    smith apple, diced
3 teaspoons raw (demerara) sugar

THE NOODLES

Preheat the oven to 180°C (350°F/Gas 4). Cook the noodles in boiling salted water according to the packet directions until they're *al dente*. Drain.

THE BASE AND COOKING

Combine all of the base ingredients together, including the drained noodles, and transfer the mixture to a large baking dish lined with baking paper. Spread the diced apple over the noodles and sprinkle the sugar over the top. Cover with foil and bake for about 45 minutes. Remove the sheet of foil 10 minutes before the end of cooking.

SLOPPY JOE

*A kids' favourite, the sloppy Joe
can, as its name suggests,
be a messy experience.
All the better!*

MAKES 6 SANDWICHES

Preparation time: 25 minutes
Cooking time: about 1 hour

INGREDIENTS

500 g (1 lb 2 oz) lean minced (ground)
    meat such as sirloin
1 onion, finely chopped
3 garlic cloves, crushed
1 green capsicum (pepper), seeded and diced
350 ml (12 fl oz) tomato passata (puréed tomatoes)
60 ml (2 fl oz/¼ cup) ketchup (page 264)
1 teaspoon Worcestershire sauce
3 teaspoons light brown sugar
1 teaspoon mustard
125 ml (4 fl oz/½ cup) water
1 teaspoon salt & 1 pinch black pepper
3 drops Tabasco® sauce
6 hot dog buns (page 102)

THE MEAT

Heat a frying pan over medium heat. Add the
minced meat and onion to the pan and cook for
10 minutes, breaking up the lumps with a spatula.
The meat should be well browned and crumbly.
Add the garlic and capsicum and cook for a further
3 minutes. Add the tomato passata, ketchup,
Worcestershire sauce, sugar and mustard. Then add
the water, salt, pepper and Tabasco®. When the sauce
starts to boil, reduce the heat as low as possible and
simmer for about 40 minutes, stirring regularly.

THE SANDWICH

Serve hot in a hot dog (or hamburger) bun.

THE ONION RINGS

See recipe page 265.

KNISH

*These stuffed buns were brought to New York by immigrants
from Eastern Europe in the early 1900s.*

MAKES 7 KNISHES

Preparation time: 40 minutes
Cooking time: 1 hour 10 minutes

FILLING

320 g (11¼ oz) potatoes,
    cut into cubes
1 brown onion, finely chopped
1½ tablespoons cooking oil
3 teaspoons matzo meal or
    ordinary breadcrumbs
3 pinches sugar
1 egg, beaten (set 2 teaspoons
aside for glazing)

DOUGH

190 g (6¾ oz) plain (all-
    purpose) flour
1 teaspoon baking powder
1½ tablespoons sunflower oil
1 egg
45 ml (1½ fl oz) water
2 pinches salt

THE FILLING

Place the potatoes in a saucepan of cold water, bring to the boil,
then lower the heat and simmer for 20 minutes until they are quite
tender. Drain. Meanwhile, sauté the onion in the oil over medium
heat for 5–10 minutes until softened and lightly brown. Mash the
potatoes and onion with the oil using a fork and incorporate the
breadcrumbs, sugar and beaten egg. Season with salt and pepper.

THE DOUGH

Using a food processor or by hand, mix until until combined.

SHAPING AND COOKING

Preheat the oven to 180°C (350°F/Gas 4). On a floured surface, roll
out the dough into a rectangular shape about 28 cm (11¼ inches)
long and 5 mm (¼ inch) thick. Spread the filling in a sausage
shape along the length of the rectangle, then roll the dough
over the sausage and pinch the ends of the tube to close it.
With the side of your hand or a chopstick, make six dents
along the length of the sausage. Separate the portions using
a knife or dough cutter. You obtain seven sections that are
open on both sides. Pinch one end closed and reshape the
knish so it's round (it will have been put out of shape by the
cutting). Pinch the sides at the other end towards the centre,
leaving a small opening (this is the top of the knish). Place the
shaped knishes on a baking tray lined with baking paper.
Brush the tops with the reserved egg and bake for
about 40 minutes until golden brown.

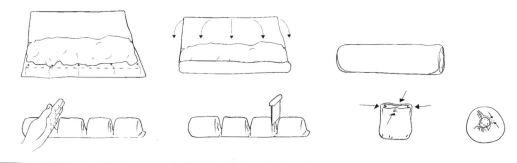

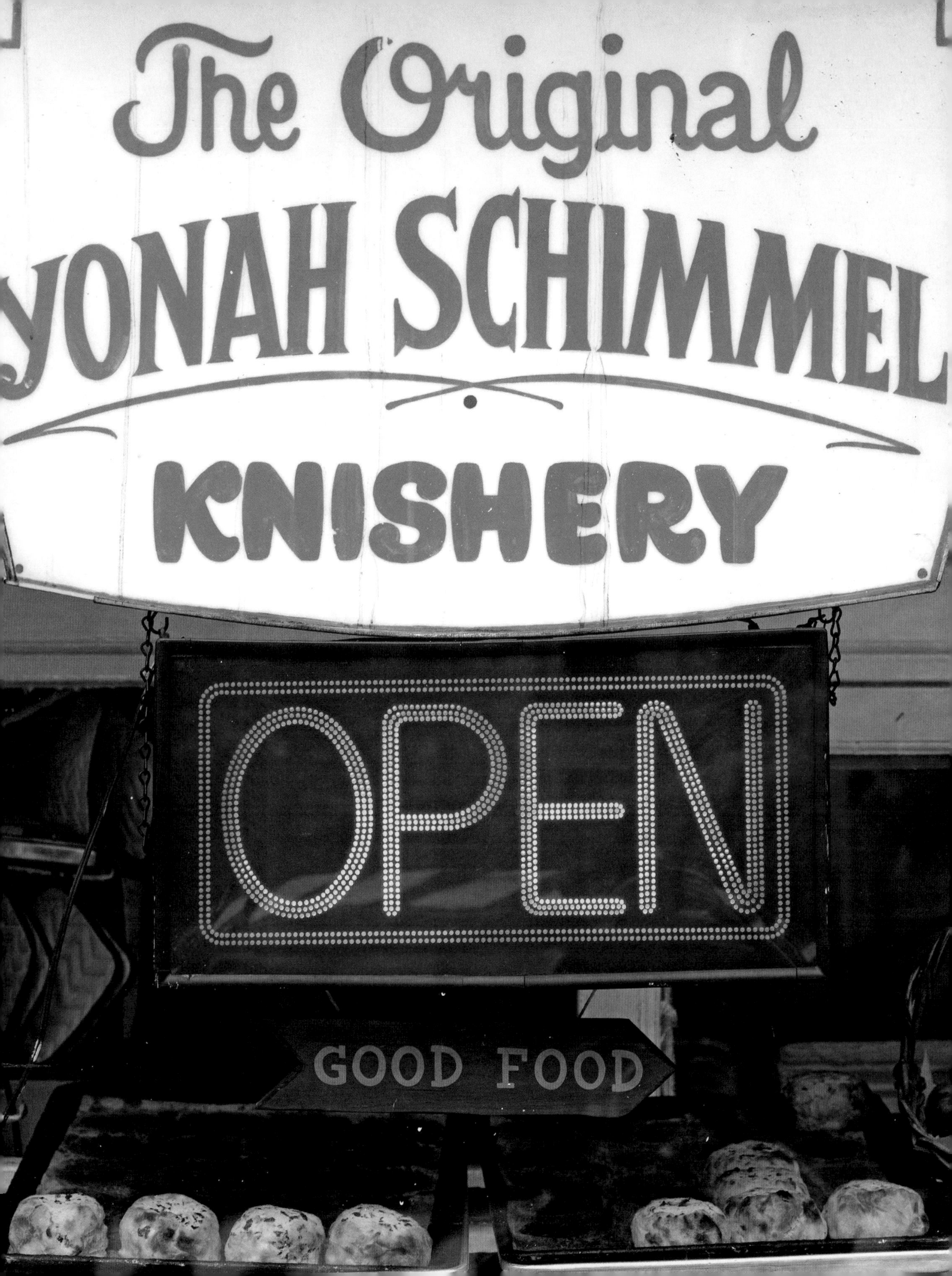
The Original
YONAH SCHIMMEL
KNISHERY
OPEN
GOOD FOOD

STUFFED CABBAGE

My grandmother, Minnie Grossman made this amazing sweet-and-sour stuffed cabbage. She showed me how to make it once, but nothing was written down and for years I've been trying to figure out the recipe. This is not far off.

SERVES 5–6

Preparation time: 30 minutes
Cooking time: 1 hour 45 minutes

INGREDIENTS

1 green cabbage

STUFFING

250 g (9 oz) minced (ground) beef
250 g (9 oz) minced (ground) veal
50 g (1¾ oz/¼ cup) jasmine rice
½ teaspoon salt
1 pinch ground black pepper
1 egg, beaten

SAUCE

200 ml (7 fl oz) tomato passata
  (puréed tomatoes)
200 ml (7 fl oz) cranberry juice
100 g (3½ oz/½ cup, lightly
  packed) light brown sugar
100 g (3½ oz) dried fruit
  (figs, raisins …)

THE CABBAGE

Boil the cabbage whole in a large pot of water for about 15 minutes until the leaves are pliable. Drain and allow to cool. Remove 10–12 large leaves to use for the cabbage rolls. Trim down the thick ribs at the base of the cabbage leaves so they can be rolled without breaking.

STUFFING AND FOLDING

Preheat the oven to 180°C (350°F/Gas 4). Mix all of the stuffing ingredients together and divide into 10–12 portions. Place each portion of meat at the bottom of a cabbage leaf and roll the leaf to enclose it, folding in the sides.

COOKING AND SERVING

Place the rolls, seam side down, in a deep roasting dish. Use some of the leftover cabbage to fill any gaps so that the rolls are packed in tight. Combine all of the sauce ingredients together and pour it over the rolls. Cover the dish with foil and cook for 1½ hours.
Leftovers can be frozen and reheated in a frying pan with a little water. For some reason, I always had the impression my grandmother's stuffed cabbage was even better thawed and reheated than it was fresh.

KNISHES

See recipe page 158.

MEATLOAF & GRAVY

A retro classic of American diners.

SERVES 6

Preparation time: 30 minutes
Cooking time: 1 hour 15 minutes

LOAF

70 g (2½ oz) celery, finely chopped
70 g (2½ oz) onion, finely chopped
70 g (2½ oz) mushrooms,
   thinly sliced
1½ tablespoons cooking oil
350 g (12 oz) minced (ground) beef
350 g (12 oz) minced (ground) veal
3 tablespoons dry breadcrumbs
125 ml (4 fl oz/½ cup) ketchup
   (page 264) + 50 ml (1¾
   fl oz), to brush over the loaf
2 teaspoons Tabasco®
   sauce (optional)
1 egg, beaten
1½ tablespoons flat-leaf
   (Italian) parsley, chopped
2 pinches salt +1 pinch
   ground black pepper

MASHED POTATOES

1 kg (2 lb 4 oz) russet
   (idaho) potatoes
70 g (2½ oz) butter
80 ml (2½ fl oz/⅓ cup) milk

GRAVY

1½ tablespoons finely
   chopped onion
50 g (1¾ oz) mushrooms,
   thinly sliced
40 g (1½ oz) butter
1½ tablespoons plain (all-
   purpose) flour
250 ml (9 fl oz/1 cup) beef stock

THE LOAF

Preheat the oven to 180°C (350°F/Gas 4). Sauté the celery, onion and mushrooms in the oil over medium heat until they're soft. Add the rest of the loaf ingredients and mix until combined. Turn into a 20 × 10 cm (8 × 4 inch) loaf (bar) tin, smooth the top, spread over the extra ketchup and cook for 1 hour.

THE MASHED POTATOES

Cut the potatoes into pieces of the same size. Place them in a saucepan of cold salted water. Bring to the boil and cook for about 15 minutes until the potatoes are tender. Drain.
Melt the butter in the milk in a saucepan over medium heat. Mash together the hot potatoes and the hot milk–butter mixture using a food processor, potato masher or a fork followed by a whisk. Season with salt and pepper. Add more milk if the mash is too dry. Serve hot.

THE GRAVY

In a saucepan, sauté the onion and mushrooms with 3 teaspoons of the butter until softened. Remove from the saucepan and set aside. Heat the remaining butter in the same saucepan. After a few minutes, when the butter starts to foam, add the flour. Stir constantly until the roux turns a light brown colour. Slowly pour in the beef stock, stirring constantly. When the mixture is smooth, increase the heat and bring to the boil. Add the mushrooms and onion and continue to cook, stirring, until it has the right consistency.

tip: the beef stock can be replaced by a stock cube dissolved
in 250 ml (9 fl oz/1 cup) boiling water.

CORNED BEEF

Making a good corned beef brisket like the one in the famous Katz sandwiches is easy, but it does take time.

MAKES ABOUT 6 SERVINGS

Preparation time: 15 minutes
Resting time: 5 days to 3 weeks
Cooking time: 4 hours

CORNING SPICES

2 teaspoons whole allspice
2 teaspoons yellow mustard
  seeds, toasted and crushed
2 teaspoons red chilli flakes
2 teaspoons whole cloves
2 teaspoons mixed peppercorns,
  toasted and crushed
2 teaspoons cardamom pods, bruised
2 bay leaves
1 teaspoon ground ginger
1 cinnamon stick, broken into pieces
2 blades of mace

CORNING LIQUID

1.5 litres (52 fl oz/6 cups)
  distilled water
115 g (4 oz) coarse non-iodised salt
1 teaspoon potassium
  nitrate (saltpetre)
2 garlic cloves

MEAT

750 g (1 lb 10 oz) beef brisket

THE CORNING SPICES

Combine all the spices together. Set aside half for the cooking liquid; the other half will be used for cooking the meat.

THE CORNING LIQUID

In a large pot, bring all the corning liquid ingredients and the half portion of the corning spices to the boil. Once the salt has completely dissolved, turn off the heat and allow the liquid to cool to room temperature, then refrigerate it. This can be done the day before.

THE CORNING

Inside a large ziplock bag, submerge the meat in the corning liquid. Squeeze as much air as possible out of the bag. Check that the meat is completely submerged and place the bag in a dish in the refrigerator for 5 days to 3 weeks, turning it once or twice a day to ensure that the meat marinates evenly.

COOKING

Rinse the meat off and place it in a flameproof casserole dish or soup pot. Add the other half of the corning spices and add water until the meat is at least 3 cm (1¼ inches) under the surface of the liquid. Bring the water to the boil, then reduce the heat to low. Simmer for 3–4 hours until the meat is very tender. You can serve the corned beef immediately, but for sandwiches it is usually best to wrap and refrigerate it first before slicing.

SPAGHETTI & MEATBALLS

Nothing fancy here. Big, authentic meatballs, a generous smothering of home-made tomato sauce, a little grated parmesan on top and some garlic bread. Good old-fashioned American–Italian food.

SERVES 4

Preparation time: 30 minutes
Cooking time: 1 hour

MEATBALLS

250 g (9 oz) minced (ground) beef
250 g (9 oz) minced (ground) pork
2 garlic cloves, crushed
1 egg, beaten
50 g (1¾ oz) parmesan
  cheese, grated
50 g (1¾ oz) fresh breadcrumbs
1 tablespoon flat-leaf (Italian)
  parsley, finely chopped
100 ml (3½ fl oz) milk
½ teaspoon salt
1 pinch ground black pepper

TOMATO SAUCE

2 tablespoons finely chopped onion
1 tablespoon each of finely
  chopped carrot and celery
45 ml (1½ fl oz) olive oil
5 garlic cloves, crushed
2 pinches dried oregano (or basil)
500 ml (17 fl oz/2 cups) tomato
  passata (puréed tomatoes)
100 ml (3½ fl oz) water

GARLIC BREAD

1 baguette (not too thin)
100 g (3½ oz) butter, softened
1½ tablespoons olive oil
3 garlic cloves, crushed
1 tablespoon flat-leaf (Italian)
  parsley, finely chopped

OTHER INGREDIENTS

400 g (14 oz) spaghetti

THE MEATBALLS

Preheat the oven to 200°C (400°F/Gas 6). Mix all of the ingredients together until combined and form 10–12 large meatballs with your hands. Arrange them on a baking tray lined with baking paper. Bake for 15 minutes.

THE TOMATO SAUCE

Meanwhile, sauté the onion, carrot and celery in the olive oil over medium heat for about 5 minutes until the onion is translucent. Stir in the crushed garlic and cook for another minute before adding the oregano, tomato passata and water. Simmer for 15 minutes. Season with salt and pepper, and a pinch of raw (demerara) sugar if you like. Add the meatballs and simmer for 15 minutes just before serving.

THE GARLIC BREAD

Preheat the oven to 180°C (350°F/Gas 4). Split the baguette in half lengthways. Mix all the other ingredients into a paste. Spread this mixture on the cut sides of the bread and place the two halves on a baking tray with the buttered sides up. Bake for about 10 minutes until they're slightly browned. Slice and serve with the dish.

SPAGHETTI

While you're making the garlic bread, start cooking the spaghetti. Cook in boiling salted water until *al dente*, then drain and serve with the meatballs and tomato sauce. Offer garlic bread on the side.

CHOLENT

This traditional Shabbat lunchtime stew is cooked for 15 hours.
As the song goes, 'Good things come to those who wait!'

SERVES 5

Preparation time: 30 minutes
Cooking time: 15 hours

INGREDIENTS

1.25 kg (2 lb 12 oz) beef short ribs
or other stewing beef
60 ml (2 fl oz/¼ cup) olive oil
1 tablespoon salt
2 brown onions, finely chopped
12 garlic cloves, finely chopped
60 g (2¼ oz) honey
3 teaspoons smoked paprika
1 teaspoon ground black pepper
200 g (7 oz) black-eyed beans, rinsed
100 g (3½ oz) whole wheat, rinsed
500 g (1 lb 2 oz) carrots, quartered
500 g (1 lb 2 oz) turnips, halved
(or left whole if small)
1.5 litres (52 fl oz/6 cups) cold
water (enough to cover the meat
by at least 5 cm/2 inches)

THE STEW

Preheat the oven to 100°C (200°F/Gas ½). Cut the meat into big evenly sized chunks and brown in 2 tablespoons of the oil with 2 teaspoons of the salt in a flameproof casserole dish over high heat. Remove the browned meat, add the rest of the oil and sauté the onions and garlic for a few minutes. Add the honey, paprika, pepper and remaining salt. Return the meat to the pot and coat with the sauce. Add the black-eyed beans, wheat, carrots and turnips and cover with cold water. Bring to the boil, remove the scum from the surface and cover with a tight-fitting lid.

COOKING IN THE OVEN

Place the casserole dish in the oven and cook for 15 hours. Usually, this is done overnight. In the morning or halfway through the cooking time, check that the meat is still covered with water and, if necessary, add more water so that the water level is at least 3 cm (1¼ inches) above the meat.

16 : 23

SNACK TIME

PB&J (PEANUT BUTTER & JELLY)

This all-American snack will be as mediocre or as fantastic as the ingredients you use.

MAKES 1 SANDWICH

Preparation time: 2 minutes

INGREDIENTS

2 slices wholemeal (whole-wheat) sandwich bread
peanut butter (page 263)
jam or jelly (pages 262–263)

Take two slices of sandwich bread. Spread peanut butter on one slice and jam or jelly on the other. Put them together. Cut and serve. That's all there is to it!

CHOCOLATE CHIP COOKIES

See recipe page 226.

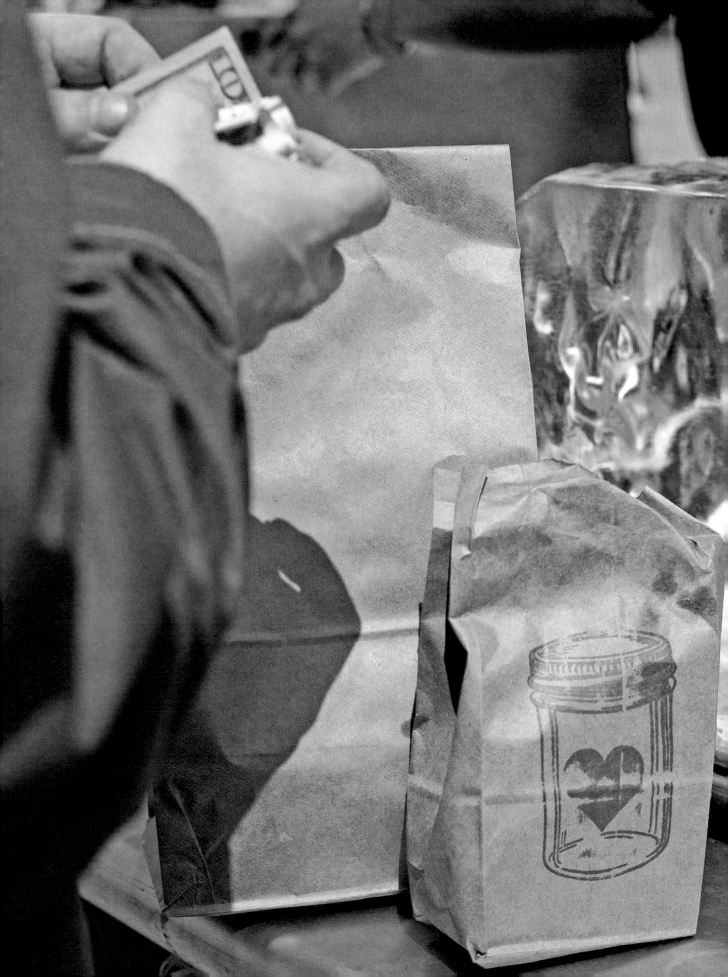

APPLE PIE

A quintessentially American experience.

MAKES 1 26 CM (10½ INCH) PIE

Preparation time: 45 minutes, plus
2 hours cooling
Resting time: 1 hour
Cooking time: about 1 hour 10 minutes

PASTRY

250 g (9 oz/1 cup) cold
    unsalted butter, diced
500 g (1 lb 2 oz/3⅓ cups)
    plain (all-purpose) flour
1 teaspoon fine salt
50 g (1¾ oz) icing (confectioners') sugar
100 ml (3½ fl oz) cold water
3 teaspoons cider vinegar

FILLING

11 small granny smith apples, peeled,
    cored and cut into small pieces
100 g (3½ oz) light brown sugar
3 teaspoons ground cinnamon
1 vanilla bean, split lengthways
    and seeds scraped
2¼ tablespoons cornflour (cornstarch)
1½ tablespoons lemon juice
    or cider vinegar
50 g (1¾ oz) unsalted butter

GLAZE

1 egg yolk
1 teaspoon water
1 tablespoon raw (demerara) sugar

THE PASTRY

Using a food processor or butter knife, cut the butter into the dry ingredients until you have a crumbly consistency. Next, incorporate the water and vinegar by hand just until you have a smooth dough. Divide into two balls of the same size, wrap them in plastic wrap and refrigerate for at least 1 hour.

THE FILLING

Combine the apple pieces with the brown sugar, cinnamon and vanilla bean seeds. Blend the cornflour with the lemon juice or cider vinegar. Heat the butter in a large frying pan over medium heat. When it starts to sizzle, add the apples and cook them until they're lightly browned on all sides — you may need to do this in batches. Add the cornflour and lemon juice mixture and continue to cook for 5 minutes, stirring. Remove from the heat and cool.

SHAPING AND BLIND BAKING

Preheat the oven to 180°C (350°F/Gas 4). If the pastry dough is too hard when it comes out of the refrigerator, let it soften. Butter and flour a 26 cm (10½ inch) pie dish.
On a floured surface, roll out the balls of dough into two rounds large enough to hang over the edge of the dish by about 5 cm (2 inches). Place one of the rounds in the dish, then roll the overhang onto itself. Prick the pastry base with a fork, cover with baking paper and dried beans and bake for 15 minutes. Remove the paper and beans and return to the oven for about 5 minutes until dry and light golden.

COOKING AND SERVING

Pour the apple filling over the baked base. Cover with the second round of pastry dough, seal the edges by pinching them together with your fingers and make small incisions on the top to let the pie breathe. Brush the pastry with the mixture of egg yolk and water, then sprinkle with the sugar. Place in the oven and bake for about 45 minutes. Allow the pie to cool for 2 hours before cutting. Serve warm with a scoop of ice cream (my preference) or cold with whipped cream (page 263).

PECAN PIE

This pecan pie has a chocolate pie crust. You will not be disappointed.

MAKES 1 26 CM (10½ INCH) PIE

Preparation time: 40 minutes, plus cooling
Resting time: 2 hours
Cooking time: about 1 hour 15 minutes

PASTRY

125 g (4½ oz/½ cup) cold
    unsalted butter, diced
225 g (8 oz/1½ cups) plain
    (all-purpose) flour
2 scant tablespoons cocoa powder
½ teaspoon fine salt
1½ tablespoons icing (confectioners') sugar
2 teaspoons vanilla sugar
60 ml (2 fl oz/¼ cup) cold water

FILLING

250 g (9 oz/2½ cups) pecans
225 ml (7¾ fl oz) sugar syrup*
340 g (11¾ oz) light brown sugar (or
    320 g/11¼ oz caster (superfine)
    sugar + 1 tablespoon molasses)
2 pinches salt
70 g (2½ oz) unsalted butter
1½ teaspoons natural vanilla extract
115 ml (3¾ fl oz) thin (pouring) cream
6 eggs

FINISHES

1 tablespoon sugar syrup*

*To make sugar syrup, combine
220 g (7¾ oz/1 cup) sugar with
250 ml (9 fl oz/1 cup) water in a
saucepan and stir over low heat until
the sugar dissolves. Bring to the
boil and remove from the heat.

THE PASTRY

Using a food processor or butter knife, cut the butter into the dry ingredients until you have a crumbly consistency. Next, incorporate the water by hand just until you have a smooth dough. Roll into a ball, wrap it in plastic wrap and refrigerate for at least 1 hour.

THE FILLING

Spread the pecans on a baking tray lined with baking paper and bake them at 180°C (350°F/Gas 4) for 10 minutes to lightly toast them. Allow them to cool for a few minutes, then crush them coarsely. In a saucepan, heat the sugar syrup, sugar, salt, butter and vanilla. Allow the sugar to dissolve on a low heat, then bring to the boil. Remove from the heat and add the cream. Stir and allow to cool. Add the eggs, one at a time, taking care to whisk the mixture well after adding each egg.

SHAPING AND BLIND BAKING

Preheat the oven to 180°C (350°F/Gas 4). If the pastry dough is too hard when it comes out of the refrigerator, let it soften. Butter and flour a 26 cm (10½ inch) pie dish. On a floured surface, roll out the dough to make a round large enough to hang over the edge of the dish by about 3 cm (1¼ inches). Place the round of dough in the dish, then roll the overhang onto itself and pinch with your fingers to stick the dough together. Let it rest in the refrigerator for at least 1 hour. Prick the pastry base with a fork, cover with baking paper and dried beans and bake for 15 minutes. Remove the paper and beans and return to the oven for about 5 minutes until dry and light golden.

COOKING AND SERVING

Spread the pecans over the baked pastry base and pour over the filling mixture. Place the pie in the oven and bake for about 40 minutes. The filling should be set but still a little wobbly in the centre. When you take it out of the oven, brush the edge of the pastry with sugar syrup. Allow to cool before cutting. Serve with a scoop of ice cream.

CHERRY PIE

Some things in life are actually as good as they appear …

MAKES 1 26 CM (10½ INCH) PIE

Preparation time: 35 minutes, plus
4 hours cooling
Resting time: about 1 hour
Cooking time: about 1 hour 20 minutes

PASTRY

250 g (9 oz/1 cup) cold
    unsalted butter, diced
500 g (1 lb 2 oz/3⅓ cups) plain
    (all-purpose) flour
50 g (1¾ oz) icing (confectioners') sugar
1 teaspoon fine salt
100 ml (3½ fl oz) cold water
3 teaspoons lemon juice

FILLING

2¼ tablespoons cornflour (cornstarch)
2¼ tablespoons lemon juice
900 g (2 lb) sour cherries, pitted
200 g (7 oz) granny smith apple,
    cored and diced, not peeled
175 g (6 oz) caster (superfine) sugar

GLAZE

1 egg yolk
a little water
raw (demerara) sugar, for sprinkling

THE PASTRY

Using a food processor or butter knife, cut the butter into
the dry ingredients until you have a crumbly consistency.
Incorporate the water and lemon juice by hand just until you
have a smooth dough. Divide into two balls of the same size,
wrap them in plastic wrap and refrigerate for at least 1 hour.

THE FILLING

Meanwhile, combine the cornflour with the lemon juice.
Place this mixture and the cherries, apple pieces and sugar
in a saucepan over medium heat. Cook together for about
15 minutes, stirring. Allow to cool completely.

SHAPING AND BLIND BAKING

Preheat the oven to 180°C (350°F/Gas 4). If the pastry
dough is too hard when it comes out of the refrigerator, let
it soften. Butter and flour a 26 cm (10½ inch) pie dish.
On a floured surface, roll out the balls of dough into two rounds large
enough to hang over the edge of the dish by about 5 cm (2 inches).
Place one of the rounds in the dish, then roll the overhang onto itself.
Prick the pastry base with a fork, cover with baking paper and dried
beans and bake for 15 minutes. Remove the paper and beans and
return to the oven for about 5 minutes until dry and light golden.
Fill the pastry shell with the cold filling. It is essential for the
filling to be cold before attempting the lattice, otherwise the
heat will make the strips of dough too soft to handle.

THE LATTICE

On a floured surface, cut the second round of dough into eight
wide strips. Lay four strips across the pie, evenly spaced. Peel
back two 'odd' strips and lay down the first of the perpendicular
strips so it's under the 'odd' strips and over the 'even' strips.
Repeat the process, peeling back the 'even' strips this time
for the second perpendicular strip to go under, and keep
going in the same way with the last two perpendicular strips,
continuing the alternation. Pinch the edges to seal them.

COOKING AND SERVING

Brush the pastry with the mixture of egg yolk and water and sprinkle
with the sugar. Place in the oven and bake for about 45 minutes.
Allow the pie to cool for at least 4 hours before cutting.

HONEY PIE

A tribute to the perfect honey and butter pie from Four & Twenty Blackbirds in Williamsburg.

MAKES 1 26 CM (10½ INCH) PIE

Preparation time: 40 minutes, plus cooling
Resting time: 1 hour
Cooking time: about 1 hour

PASTRY

125 g (4½ oz/½ cup) cold
   unsalted butter, diced
235 g (8½ oz) plain (all-purpose) flour
25 g (1 oz) icing (confectioners') sugar
½ teaspoon fine salt
55 ml (1¾ fl oz) cold water
1 teaspoon cider vinegar
1 egg, beaten

FILLING

2¼ tablespoons fine polenta (cornmeal)
4½ teaspoons cider vinegar
1 teaspoon natural vanilla extract
6 eggs
125 ml (4 fl oz/½ cup) thin
   (pouring) cream
1 pinch salt
80 g (2¾ oz) unsalted butter
300 g (10½ oz) light brown sugar
   (or 280 g/10 oz caster (superfine)
   sugar + 3 teaspoons molasses)
80 ml (2½ fl oz/⅓ cup) sugar
   syrup (page 176)
100 g (3½ oz) acacia or other light honey
4½ teaspoons fine sea salt

THE PASTRY

Using a food processor, cut the butter into the flour, icing sugar and salt, then incorporate the water and vinegar by hand just until you have a smooth dough. Roll into a ball, wrap it in plastic wrap and refrigerate for 1 hour.

SHAPING AND BLIND BAKING

Preheat the oven to 180°C (350°F/Gas 4). If the pastry dough is too hard when it comes out of the refrigerator, let it soften. Butter and flour a 26 cm (10½ inch) pie dish. On a floured surface, roll out the dough into a round large enough to hang over the edge of the dish by about 3 cm (1¼ inches). Place the round of dough in the dish, then roll the overhang onto itself and pinch with your fingers to shape the edge. Prick the pastry base with a fork, cover with baking paper and dried beans and bake for 15 minutes. Remove the paper and beans and brush the base with the beaten egg. Return to the oven for 2 minutes until dry and light golden, lowering the temperature to 170°C (325°F/Gas 3).

THE FILLING

Combine the polenta, vinegar, vanilla, eggs, cream and salt. In a pan, bring the butter, sugar, sugar syrup and honey to the boil. Lower the heat and stir in the egg mixture, mixing with a spatula for about 5 minutes until you have a smooth cream. Do not boil.

ASSEMBLY AND COOKING

Preheat the oven to 180°C (350°F/Gas 4). Pour the filling into the pre-cooked pie shell. Bake for about 40 minutes until the filling is set, but still a little wobbly. Allow to cool and sprinkle with the fine sea salt.

PUMPKIN PIE

This smooth, delicious interpretation of the Thanksgiving classic is a gift from my friend Sara Jane Crawford, who has lent her baking skills to such fine establishments as the Rose Bakery in Paris and Marlow & Sons in Brooklyn.

MAKES 1 26 CM (10½ INCH) PIE

Preparation time: 30 minutes, plus cooling
Resting time: 1 hour
Cooking time: about 1 hour 40 minutes

PASTRY

135 g (4¾ oz) cold unsalted butter, diced
210 g (7½ oz) plain (all-purpose) flour
½ teaspoon fine salt
70 ml (2¼ fl oz) cold water
1 teaspoon lemon juice
1 egg, beaten

FILLING

3 eggs
1 egg yolk
120 g (4¼ oz) light brown sugar
   (or 115 g/4 oz caster (superfine)
   sugar + 1 teaspoon molasses)
125 ml (4 fl oz/½ cup) maple syrup
350 ml (12 fl oz) thin (pouring) cream
415 g (14¾ oz) pumpkin purée*
1 teaspoon ground cinnamon
1 teaspoon ground ginger
½ teaspoon ground nutmeg

*You can use shop-bought frozen pumpkin purée, thawed, or make your own purée according to Sara's instructions.

THE PASTRY

Using a food processor, cut the butter into the flour and salt until the mixture is crumbly, then incorporate the water and lemon juice by hand just until you have a smooth dough. Roll into a ball, wrap it in plastic wrap and refrigerate for 1 hour.

SHAPING AND BLIND BAKING

Preheat the oven to 170°C (325°F/Gas 3). If the pastry dough is too hard when it comes out of the refrigerator, let it soften. Butter and flour a 26 cm (10½ inch) pie dish.
On a floured surface, roll out the dough into a round large enough to hang over the edge of the dish by about 3 cm (1¼ inches).
Place the round of dough in the dish, then roll the overhang onto itself and pinch with your fingers to shape the edge. Cover the pastry with baking paper and dried beans and bake for about 40 minutes until the edges are golden and the pastry is quite dry. Remove the paper and beans and brush the base with the beaten egg. Return to the oven for 2 minutes until dry and light golden.

THE FILLING

Preheat the oven to 180°C (350°F/Gas 4). Whisk together the eggs, egg yolk and sugar. Incorporate the rest of the filling ingredients one by one and mix until combined. Pour the filling into the pastry shell and bake for about 40 minutes until the filling has set. Allow to cool before serving.

FOR HOME-MADE PUMPKIN PURÉE

Preheat the oven to 220°C (425°F/Gas 7). Peel a butternut pumpkin (about 450 g/1 lb before cooking), remove the seeds and cut into pieces. Place on a baking tray lined with baking paper, add enough water to cover the paper and bake for about 1 hour, until the pumpkin flesh is very soft. Let the pieces of pumpkin cool, then process them until you have a quite smooth purée. If it is too watery, let it drain overnight in the refrigerator in a colander lined with a clean cotton tea towel (dish towel).

CHINESE EGG CUSTARD TARTS

Warm custard tarts straight out of the steam oven are a staple of Chinatown coffee shops.
For the authentic shiny egg custard, you need to bake it slowly at a low temperature.

MAKES ABOUT 30 SMALL TARTS

Preparation time: 30 minutes
Resting time: 2–3 hours
Cooking time: 40 minutes

INNER 'FAT' PASTRY

175 g (6 oz) unsalted
    butter, softened
175 g (6 oz) coconut oil,
    soft or melted
250 g (9 oz/1⅔ cups) plain
    (all-purpose) flour

OUTER EGG PASTRY

250 g (9 oz/1⅔ cups) plain
    (all-purpose) flour
1 egg
80 ml (2½ fl oz/⅓ cup) iced water

FOR THE CUSTARD

150 g (5½ oz/⅔ cup) sugar
375 ml (13 fl oz/1½ cups) water
3 teaspoons cornflour (cornstarch)
85 ml (2¾ fl oz) evaporated milk
4 eggs
4 egg yolks

THE PASTRIES

Combine all of the inner 'fat' pastry ingredients together
into a dough and refrigerate for 30 minutes.
Do the same for the outer egg pastry and refrigerate for 30 minutes as well.

SHAPING AND FOLDING

On a floured surface, roll out the first dough into a 20 cm (8 inch)
square, then roll out the egg dough into a 30 cm (12 inch) square.
Place the smaller pastry square in the middle of the egg pastry square,
so that the edges of the inside square are at a 45° angle to the edges of
the outer square. Fold in the corners of the outer square over the inner
square. Pinch the seams of the outer dough closed. Rest in the refrigerator
for 30 minutes, then roll out the combined dough into a long rectangle,
5 mm (¼ inch) thick, making sure that the top and bottom edges of the
rectangle are parallel to the rolling pin. Fold in each end like an envelope
and return the dough to the refrigerator for another 30 minutes. Repeat
the process two to four times, resting the pastry each time for 30 minutes.
Grease and flour 30 small tart (flan) tins approximately 6 cm (2½ inches)
along the base and 9 cm (3½ inches) in diameter (disposable mince pie
foil cases or similar are ideal). To finish, roll out the pastry to a thickness
of 5 mm (¼ inch) and use a cutter to cut out circles that are large enough
to line the tins. Place the circles of pastry into the tins and refrigerate.

THE CUSTARD

Preheat the oven to 180°C (350°F/Gas 4). In a saucepan, dissolve
the sugar in the water over low heat and let it cool for 5 minutes.
Blend the cornflour with 1 tablespoon of the evaporated milk,
then mix in the rest of the evaporated milk, the eggs and the yolks.
Whisk this mixture into the sugar water until combined.

COOKING

Place the tins lined with pastry on a baking tray, fill them with the custard
and bake, lowering the oven temperature to 150°C (300°F/Gas 2).
Cook for 35 minutes until the filling is set but still a little wobbly.

Pastries + Food

Savory pies 6⁰⁰/7⁰⁰
Scones 3⁰⁰
Savory brioche 4⁰⁰
Savory bread 2⁵⁰
blackbird's bread 2⁵⁰
muffins 3⁰⁰
cinnamon brioche 3⁰⁰
blackbird's granola
w/milk 4⁰⁰ w/yogurt 4⁵⁰
egg in a nest 4⁵⁰

SPE
on
SMOK
w/
Ro
SW

CARROT CAKE

A cold slice of moist, spiced carrot cake, with a thick topping of cream cheese frosting. What could be better?

MAKES 1 22 CM (8½ INCH) CAKE

Preparation time: 30 minutes, plus cooling
Cooking time: 40 minutes

WET INGREDIENTS

135 g (4¾ oz) light brown sugar (or
    120 g/4¼ oz caster (superfine)
    sugar + 2 teaspoons molasses)
125 ml (4 fl oz/½ cup) sunflower oil
4 eggs
1½ tablespoons orange juice
zest of 1 orange, finely grated
1 teaspoon natural vanilla extract

DRY INGREDIENTS

235 g (8½ oz) plain (all-purpose) flour
2 teaspoons baking powder
3 pinches salt
2 teaspoons ground cinnamon
4 pinches grated nutmeg
4 pinches ground cardamom
4 pinches freshly ground black pepper

CARROTS, FRUIT AND NUTS

235 g (8½ oz) carrot, grated
2 tablespoons raisins
2 tablespoons chopped walnuts

FROSTING

100 g (3½ oz) unsalted butter, softened
150 g (5½ oz) plain cream cheese, softened
(25% dairy fat, such as Philadelphia®)
100 g (3½ oz) icing (confectioners') sugar
100 g (3½ oz) desiccated (shredded)
    coconut (optional)

THE BATTER

Preheat the oven to 180°C (350°F/Gas 4). Beat the wet ingredients together vigorously. Combine the dry ingredients and add them to the wet mixture without overworking the batter. Finally, incorporate the carrots, fruit and nuts. Butter and flour a 22 cm (8½ inch) cake tin. Pour in the batter and smooth the top.

COOKING

Bake for about 40 minutes until a skewer inserted into the middle of the cake comes out clean. Allow to cool.

THE FROSTING

Process the butter, cream cheese and sugar in an electric mixer or beat with a wooden spoon until smooth and combined. Spread the frosting on the cake using a knife or spatula. Scatter over the desiccated coconut, if using.

APPLE STRUDEL & CHERRY–RICOTTA STRUDEL

The flaky, buttery layers are the key to this traditional dessert from Central Europe.

MAKES 1 STRUDEL

Preparation time: 45 minutes, plus cooling
Cooking time: about 35 minutes

APPLE STRUDEL

40 g (1½ oz) unsalted butter
5 granny smith apples, peeled,
    cored and diced (about 375
    g/13 oz prepared apple)
75 g (2¾ oz/⅓ cup) caster
    (superfine) sugar
2 teaspoons finely grated lemon zest
50 g (1¾ oz/½ cup) flaked almonds
1 teaspoon natural vanilla extract
1½ teaspoons cornflour (cornstarch)
1½ tablespoons lemon juice

CHERRY–RICOTTA STRUDEL

400 g (14 oz) ricotta cheese
60 g (2¼ oz) caster (superfine) sugar
5 teaspoons cornflour (cornstarch)
2 egg whites
175 g (6 oz) frozen sour cherries,
    thawed or 175 g (6 oz) fresh
    cherries, pitted and halved
85 g (3 oz) plain (all-purpose) flour

PASTRY FOR ONE STRUDEL

50 g (1¾ oz) dry breadcrumbs
95 g (3¼ oz) caster (superfine) sugar
1½ teaspoons ground cinnamon
    for the apple strudel or 1 vanilla
    bean, split lengthways and seeds
    scraped, for the cherry strudel
4 sheets filo pastry
100 g (3½ oz) unsalted butter, melted

THE APPLE STRUDEL FILLING

Heat the butter in a frying pan over medium–high heat. At the first sizzle, add the apple and sugar. Sauté for 3 minutes. Add the lemon zest, almonds and vanilla and continue cooking until the apples are lightly browned on all sides. Blend the cornflour in with the lemon juice and then add the entire mixture to the apples. Cook for another 5 minutes, stirring. Allow to cool.

THE CHERRY–RICOTTA STRUDEL FILLING

In a mixing bowl, whisk together the ricotta, sugar, cornflour and egg whites. When the mixture is smooth, warm it over low heat in a saucepan for 5 minutes to thicken it a little. Allow to cool.
Toss the cherries in the flour, then shake them a little to remove the excess.

ASSEMBLY

Preheat the oven to 200°C (400°F/Gas 6). Combine the breadcrumbs, sugar and cinnamon if making the apple strudel, or the breadcrumbs, sugar and vanilla bean seeds if making the cherry strudel.
Lay the first sheet of filo on a baking tray lined with baking paper. Brush it with melted butter and sprinkle with the breadcrumb mixture. Place another sheet on top and repeat the process with the remaining sheets of filo pastry and breadcrumb mixture, reserving a little mixture for the top.
For the apple strudel, spread out the apple filling in a sausage shape along one long side of the sheets of filo and roll up to enclose the filling.
For the cherry–ricotta strudel, spread the ricotta filling over the entire surface of the filo sheets, leaving a 3 cm (1¼ inch) border around the edges. Place two rows of the lightly floured cherries on the ricotta filling, one about one-third along the width of the filo sheets, the second two-thirds along. Roll the filo sheets up widthways to form a sausage.

COOKING

Brush the surface of the strudel with the remaining melted butter and sprinkle with the remaining breadcrumb mixture. Bake for about 22 minutes. Allow to cool and serve in slices.

NEW YORK CHEESECAKE

The genuine article, like the one you can eat at Junior's in Brooklyn.
Made with cream cheese and NOT cooked in a bain-marie.

**MAKES 1 28 CM (11¼ INCH)
CHEESECAKE**

Preparation time: 25 minutes
Cooking time: 1 hour 15 minutes
Resting time in the oven: 2 hours
Refrigeration time: 4 hours

CRUST

185 g (6½ oz) sweet wholemeal
    biscuits (e.g. Graham
    Crackers®), crushed
1 tablespoon caster (superfine) sugar
90 g (3¼ oz/⅓ cup) unsalted
    butter, melted

CHEESE FILLING

900 g (2 lb) plain cream cheese,
    softened (25% dairy fat,
    preferably Philadelphia®)
260 g (9¼ oz) caster
    (superfine) sugar
½ teaspoon salt
70 g (2½ oz) plain (all-
    purpose) flour
1 lemon, juice and finely grated zest
600 g (1 lb 5 oz) sour cream
    (30% dairy fat)
8 eggs
1 teaspoon natural vanilla extract

THE CRUST

Grease the base and side of a 28 cm (11¼ inch) spring-form cake tin. Preheat the oven to 180°C (350°F/Gas 4). Combine the crushed biscuits, sugar and melted butter, then spread this mixture over the base, pressing it down well with the bottom of a glass. Place in the oven and bake for 15 minutes. Take the crust out of the oven and increase the temperature to 230°C (450°F/Gas 8).

THE CHEESE FILLING

Using an electric mixer or food processor, combine the filling ingredients, in the order they are listed, until smooth. Pour over the crust.

COOKING

Bake for 10 minutes. Without opening the oven, lower the temperature to 100°C (200°F/Gas ½) and cook for another 50 minutes. The filling should still be a little wobbly in the centre. Turn the oven off and let the cheesecake rest inside for 2 hours, then let it cool outside of the oven and refrigerate for at least 4 hours before serving.

ITALIAN-STYLE CHEESECAKE

This is the other great New York cheesecake. Unlike its better-known rival, which is made with cream cheese, the Italian version is made with ricotta cheese, resulting in a lighter, slightly wet consistency.

MAKES TWO 12 CM (4½ INCH) CHEESECAKES

Preparation time: 25 minutes, plus cooling
Cooking time: 15 minutes

CRUST

125 g (4½ oz) plain (all-purpose) flour
½ teaspoon salt
50 g (1¾ oz) ricotta cheese
50 g (1¾ oz) unsalted butter, softened
100 g (3½ oz) icing (confectioners') sugar

CHEESE FILLING

450 g (1 lb) ricotta cheese
100 g (3½ oz) caster (superfine) sugar
25 g (1 oz) plain (all-purpose) flour
2 eggs
1 pinch salt
60 ml (2 fl oz/¼ cup) lemon juice or
   pastis (anise-flavoured liqueur)
½ teaspoon natural vanilla extract

DECORATION

100 g (3½ oz/⅔ cup) strawberries
icing (confectioners') sugar for dusting

THE CRUST

Preheat the oven to 230°C (450°F/Gas 8). Mix the ingredients for the crust using a food processor or by hand until combined. Butter and flour the base and one-third of the way up the sides of two 12 cm (4½ inch) spring-form cake tins, then spread the mixture over the base.

THE CHEESE FILLING

Whisk together the cheese filling ingredients until smooth, then pour equal amounts over the two crusts.

COOKING

Bake the cheesecakes for about 15 minutes. When they come out of the oven, the filling should still be wobbly in the centre. Allow to cool.

THE DECORATION

Arrange slices of strawberry on top of each cheesecake

CHOCOLATE CUPCAKES

The following are my three favourite cupcake recipes.
Feel free to mix and match the batter and frosting recipes in different ways.

MAKES ABOUT 18 CUPCAKES

Preparation time: 25 minutes, plus cooling
Cooking time: 20 minutes

INGREDIENTS FOR MELTING

200 g (7 oz) dark chocolate, cut into pieces
250 g (9 oz/1 cup) unsalted butter
4½ teaspoons cocoa powder

INGREDIENTS FOR WHISKING

6 eggs, separated
225 g (8 oz) caster (superfine) sugar

DRY INGREDIENTS

165 g (5¾ oz) plain (all-purpose) flour
1 pinch salt

COFFEE FROSTING

125 g (4½ oz/½ cup) unsalted
   butter, softened
225 g (8 oz) icing (confectioners') sugar
25 g (1 oz) light brown sugar
45 ml (1½ fl oz) cold espresso coffee
1 teaspoon coffee extract

THE CHOCOLATE CUPCAKE

Preheat the oven to 160°C (315°F/Gas 2–3).
In a saucepan, melt the pieces of chocolate with the butter
and cocoa powder, stirring regularly. Remove from heat.
Whisk together the egg yolks and sugar until thick and
pale. Beat the egg whites until stiff peaks form.
Combine the dry ingredients in a bowl. Gradually add the
combined dry ingredients to the egg yolk and sugar mixture. Mix
well, then pour in the melted chocolate–butter mixture while
stirring. Carefully fold in the beaten egg whites using a spatula.
Fill muffin tins with paper liners and divide the batter between
them. Cook in the oven for about 20 minutes. Allow to cool. Turn
out the cupcakes and spread frosting on each one using a spatula.

THE COFFEE FROSTING

Beat the butter and sugars together in a food processor or with a
spatula until smooth. Add the coffee and the coffee extract and mix
again vigorously in the processor or with the spatula for at least
5 minutes until the mixture becomes creamy. It is then ready to use.

VANILLA CUPCAKES

MAKES ABOUT 20 CUPCAKES

Preparation time: 20 minutes, plus cooling
Cooking time: 25 minutes

DRY INGREDIENTS

250 g (9 oz/1⅔ cups) plain (all-purpose) flour
2¼ teaspoons baking powder
1 pinch salt

INGREDIENTS FOR WHISKING

6 eggs
1½ teaspoons natural vanilla extract
1 teaspoon finely grated orange zest
250 g (9 oz/1 cup) unsalted
butter, at room temperature
225 g (8 oz) caster (superfine) sugar

VANILLA FROSTING

125 g (4½ oz/½ cup) unsalted
butter, softened
250 g (9 oz/2 cups) icing
   (confectioners') sugar
1 tablespoon milk
½ vanilla bean, split lengthways
   and seeds scraped

THE VANILLA CUPCAKE

Preheat the oven to 160°C (315°F/Gas 2–3).
Combine the dry ingredients together. Using an electric mixer, beat the eggs, vanilla and zest on a high speed until light and fluffy. Whisk the softened butter and sugar together vigorously, then alternately add the combined dry ingredients and the egg mixture. Carefully combine.
Fill silicon moulds or two muffin tins with paper liners and divide the batter between them.
Cook in the oven for about 25 minutes. Allow to cool. Turn out the cupcakes and spread frosting on each one using a spatula.

THE VANILLA FROSTING

Beat the butter and sugar together in a food processor or with a spatula until smooth. Add the milk and the vanilla bean seeds and mix again vigorously in the processor or with the spatula for at least 5 minutes. The mixture will become creamy and is then ready to use.

MATCHA CUPCAKES

MAKES ABOUT 20 CUPCAKES

Preparation time: 20 minutes, plus cooling
Cooking time: 25 minutes

DRY INGREDIENTS

250 g (9 oz/1⅔ cups) plain
   (all-purpose) flour
4½ teaspoons matcha green tea powder
2¼ teaspoons baking powder
1 pinch salt

INGREDIENTS FOR WHISKING

6 eggs
250 g (9 oz/1 cup) unsalted butter,
   at room temperature
225 g (8 oz) caster (superfine) sugar

RASPBERRY FROSTING

125 g (4½ oz) raspberry jam
125 g (4½ oz/½ cup) unsalted
   butter, softened
225 g (8 oz) icing (confectioners') sugar

THE MATCHA CUPCAKE

Preheat the oven to 160°C (315°F/Gas 2–3).
Combine the dry ingredients together. Using an electric mixer, beat
the eggs on a high speed until light and fluffy. Whisk the softened
butter and sugar together vigorously, then alternately add the
combined dry ingredients and the eggs. Carefully combine.
Fill silicon moulds or two muffin tins with paper
liners and divide the batter between them.
Cook in the oven for about 25 minutes. Allow to cool. Turn out
the cupcakes and spread frosting on each one using a spatula.

THE RASPBERRY FROSTING

Heat the raspberry jam in a small saucepan,
strain to remove the seeds, then cool.
Beat the butter and sugar together in a food processor or with a spatula until
smooth. Add the strained raspberry jam and mix again vigorously for at
least 5 minutes. The mixture will become creamy and is then ready to use.

DOODLES

For a different cupcake experience, use the batter and frosting recipes from the previous pages to make inside-out cupcakes, which we call doodles.

THE BATTER

When you make cupcakes, you try to achieve a top that's nice and flat. When you make doodles, which aren't frosted, you want them to be more rounded. To do that, I cook them in a hotter oven but for a shorter time. So it's just the cooking that's different.

CHOCOLATE DOODLES

170°C (325°F/Gas 3) for 23 minutes.

VANILLA DOODLES

170°C (325°F/Gas 3) for 24 minutes.

MATCHA DOODLES

170°C (325°F/Gas 3) for 24 minutes.

THE FROSTING

Once the doodles have cooled, make holes in the middle of the top using a chopstick or rod. Fill a piping (icing) bag fitted with a plain nozzle with frosting and fill the inside of the doodles.

FLOURLESS CHOCOLATE CAKE

The inspiration for this cake is the mousse-like chocolate cake at Diner, in Williamsburg, Brooklyn. It's an intense, light, pure chocolate experience.

MAKES 1 24 CM (9½ INCH) CAKE

Preparation time: 20 minutes, plus cooling
Cooking time: about 1 hour

INGREDIENTS

125 g (4½ oz/½ cup) unsalted butter
   + extra for greasing the tin
300 g (10½ oz) dark chocolate
1½ tablespoons cocoa powder
6 eggs, separated
100 g (3½ oz) caster (superfine)
   sugar + extra for dusting the tin
1 pinch salt
150 g (5½ oz) sour cream (30% dairy fat)
½ teaspoon natural vanilla extract

THE TIN

Preheat the oven to 150°C (300°F/Gas 2). Wrap foil around the seams of a 24 cm (9½ inch) spring-form cake tin so you can bake the cake in a bain-marie (water bath). Cover the inside of the tin with a thick layer of softened butter. Sprinkle some sugar for dusting on the butter and tilt the tin to distribute the sugar evenly, shaking out the excess.

THE MIXTURE

Melt the butter, chocolate and cocoa powder together over low heat, in a double boiler or in the microwave. Beat the egg whites with half the sugar and the salt until stiff peaks form. Beat the yolks with the remaining sugar, sour cream and vanilla until smooth. Combine the egg yolk mixture with the melted chocolate mixture, then fold in the egg white mixture until the mixture is incorporated.

COOKING AND SERVING

Pour the batter into the tin and place the tin inside a larger baking dish. Pour boiling water into the larger dish to three-quarters of the height of the cake tin. Bake for 55 minutes or until a skewer inserted into the middle of the cake comes out clean. Remove the bain-marie from the oven, leaving the cake in it for 3 more minutes. Remove the cake from the bain-marie and allow to cool. Serve chilled with whipped cream (page 263).

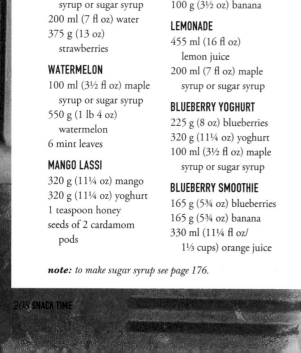

GOOD POPS

Popsicles (or Bobsicles, in this case) are the perfect summer treat. Here are a few easy and delicious fruit-based recipes from the barman/manager at Bob's Juice Bar: Jean-Pierre Ahtuam.

FOR 6 LARGE POPSICLES
Preparation time: 5 minutes
Freezing time: at least 8 hours

In each case, you simply blend everything together in a blender or food processor, as you would for a smoothie. Fill moulds with the mixture, insert popsicle sticks or handles in the top, then seal and freeze. You can use store-bought moulds with built-in handles, or use disposable cups or recycled dessert containers as moulds, as I've done for the 'bad pops', page 210. Freeze the popsicles for at least 8 hours. Take the popsicle out of the freezer to warm up for a few minutes before trying to sink your teeth into it.

STRAWBERRY
55 ml (1¾ fl oz) maple
    syrup or sugar syrup
200 ml (7 fl oz) water
375 g (13 oz)
    strawberries

WATERMELON
100 ml (3½ fl oz) maple
    syrup or sugar syrup
550 g (1 lb 4 oz)
    watermelon
6 mint leaves

MANGO LASSI
320 g (11¼ oz) mango
320 g (11¼ oz) yoghurt
1 teaspoon honey
seeds of 2 cardamom
    pods

ROCKMELON
550 g (1 lb 4 oz) melon
100 g (3½ oz) banana

LEMONADE
455 ml (16 fl oz)
    lemon juice
200 ml (7 fl oz) maple
    syrup or sugar syrup

BLUEBERRY YOGHURT
225 g (8 oz) blueberries
320 g (11¼ oz) yoghurt
100 ml (3½ fl oz) maple
    syrup or sugar syrup

BLUEBERRY SMOOTHIE
165 g (5¾ oz) blueberries
165 g (5¾ oz) banana
330 ml (11¼ fl oz/
    1⅓ cups) orange juice

note: *to make sugar syrup see page 176.*

BAD POPS

Here are two non-fruit popsicles that never fail to satisfy.

CHOCOLATE POPSICLES

MAKES 6

Preparation time: 10 minutes
Cooking time: 10 minutes
Freezing time: at least 8 hours

INGREDIENTS

1½ tablespoons cornflour
   (cornstarch)
150 ml (5 fl oz) milk
310 ml (10¾ fl oz/1¼ cups)
   thin (pouring) cream
2 pinches salt
30 g (1 oz/¼ cup) cocoa powder
90 g (3¼ oz) caster (superfine) sugar
30 g (1 oz) dark chocolate, chopped
1 teaspoon natural vanilla extract

THE CREAM

Make a slurry from the cornflour and 2 tablespoons of milk. Add the rest of the milk, mix and set aside.
In a saucepan over low heat, whisk together the cream, salt, cocoa and sugar. Reduce the heat when it starts to boil. Add the milk–cornflour mixture, continuing to whisk.
When the mixture starts to thicken, remove from the heat and mix in the chocolate pieces and vanilla. Stir until melted and smooth.

SETTING AND SERVING

Pour into popsicle moulds, cool, then secure the popsicle sticks, cover and freeze for at least 8 hours.

note: *this popsicle is also known as a 'fudgesicle'.*

COFFEE POPSICLES

MAKES 6

Preparation time: 10 minutes
Freezing time: at least 8 hours

INGREDIENTS

200 ml (7 fl oz) sweetened
   condensed milk
400 ml (14 fl oz) strong cold coffee

Whisk together the condensed milk and coffee until smooth. Pour into popsicle moulds, secure the popsicle sticks, cover and freeze for at least 8 hours.

note: *for the popsicles you see in the photo, I used take-out espresso cups with matching lids that I poked the sticks through. You could do the same thing with another home-made solution such as recycled yoghurt tubs with some foil, or use store-bought popsicle moulds with the sticks built in.*

HOME-MADE GRAHAM CRACKERS®

This honey-flavoured biscuit is a key ingredient in cheesecakes and s'mores. It is also delicious to munch on by itself.

MAKES ABOUT 32 BISCUITS

Preparation time: 20 minutes, plus cooling
Refrigeration time: at least 1 hour
Cooking time: about 15 minutes

WET INGREDIENTS

60 g (2¼ oz/¼ cup) unsalted
    butter, softened
115 g (4 oz) light brown sugar (or
    100 g/3½ oz caster (superfine)
    sugar + 2 teaspoons molasses)
1 egg
1½ tablespoons honey
1½ tablespoons milk

DRY INGREDIENTS

1 teaspoon baking powder
½ teaspoon salt
250 g (9 oz/1⅔ cups) wholemeal
    (whole-wheat) flour

THE PASTRY

Beat the butter and sugar in an electric mixer or by hand until light and creamy. Whisk together the egg, honey and milk. Combine all the dry ingredients together.
Add the egg mixture to the butter mixture alternately with the dry ingredients until you have a smooth dough. Form into a ball, cover loosely in plastic wrap and refrigerate for at least 1 hour.

SHAPING THE PASTRY

Preheat the oven to 180°C (350°F/Gas 4). Divide the dough into two balls. Roll out one ball thinly to about 2 mm (1/16 inch) thick on a baking tray lined with baking paper. Using a pastry cutter or a knife, score the rolled-out dough into 16 rectangles of the same size. Using the tip of a knife, make lines of small holes on the biscuits.

COOKING

Bake for about 15 minutes until the biscuits are golden brown. As soon as they come out of the oven, separate the biscuits using a dough cutter following the marks made before cooking. Allow to cool on the baking tray and set the biscuits aside. Repeat the process with the second ball of dough.

note: *reserve any off-cuts to crush and use as a biscuit base for cheesecakes (page 196) or tarts.*

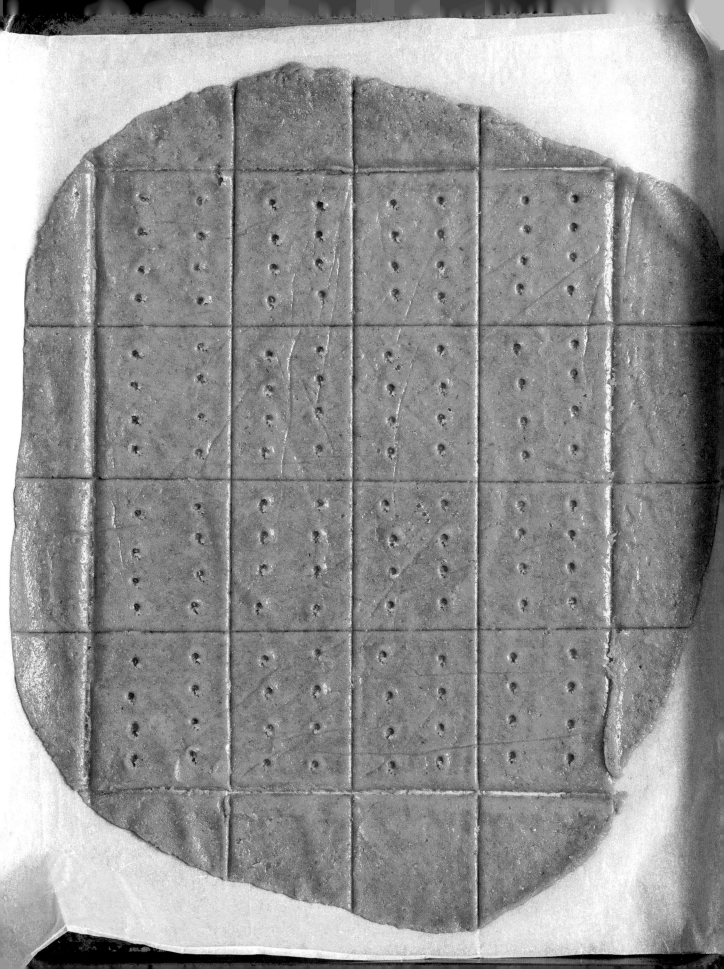

S'MORES

When I was a kid, we made s'mores at summer camp around the fire, toasting marshmallows on tree branches and then sandwiching them with chocolate between two Graham Crackers®.

MAKES 1 S'MORE

Preparation time: 5 minutes
Cooking time: 5 minutes

INGREDIENTS

2 home-made extra-large Graham Crackers® (page 212) or other sweet wholemeal biscuits
4 squares of dark chocolate (enough to cover a biscuit)
1 piece of marshmallow the size of the biscuit (page 232)

Preheat the oven grill (broiler). Place a biscuit on a baking tray lined with baking paper, top it with squares of chocolate and a piece of marshmallow the same size as the biscuit. Place under the grill and monitor the cooking carefully. After about a minute, the marshmallow starts to colour and smell like caramel and the chocolate starts to melt. When that happens, remove from under the grill, top with the second biscuit and serve immediately.

extra large Graham Crackers®:Graham Crackers®are the biscuits used for s'mores. To make extra-large s'mores, just make your home-made Graham Crackers® thicker and wider. Roll out the dough until about 5 mm (¼ inch) thick and cut into rectangles about 10 x 8 cm (4 x 3¼ inches). Cook them for 18–20 minutes until they're golden brown. Separate biscuits with a pastry cutter as soon as they come out of the oven and let them cool on a rack. You need two biscuits to make a s'more.

WHOOPIE PIES

'Makin' whoopee' means to make love, and eating these light and airy Amish cakes is effectively an ecstatic experience.

MAKES 14 WHOOPIE PIES

Preparation time: 30 minutes, plus cooling
Cooking time: 8 minutes

COOKIES

210 g (7½ oz) plain (all-purpose) flour
3 teaspoons baking powder
35 g (1¼ oz) cocoa powder
85 g (3 oz) coconut oil, at room
    temperature, or unsalted
    butter, softened
135 g (4¾ oz) light brown sugar (or
    120 g/4¼ oz caster (superfine)
    sugar + 2 teaspoons molasses)
2 egg yolks
1 pinch salt
100 ml (3½ fl oz) water

FILLING

2 egg whites
2 pinches salt
100 ml (3½ fl oz) cold sugar
    syrup (page 176)
100 g (3½ oz) icing (confectioners') sugar
1 teaspoon natural vanilla extract

THE COOKIE BATTER

Preheat the oven to 200°C (400°F/Gas 6). Combine the flour, baking powder and cocoa. In a food processor or by hand, beat the coconut oil and sugar vigorously until light and creamy. Incorporate the egg yolks, then the flour mixture, the salt and finally the water, continuing to beat until you have a smooth batter.

COOKING

Using a spoon or a piping (icing) bag fitted with a plain nozzle, pipe tablespoons of mixture on two baking trays lined with baking paper, leaving 3 cm (1¼ inches) between each. Bake for about 8 minutes until the cookies are well risen and quite firm. Allow to cool.

THE FILLING

Using an electric beater, whisk the egg whites with the salt and, when they begin to froth up, gradually incorporate the sugar syrup. When the mixture has doubled in volume, gradually add the icing sugar and the vanilla, continuing to whisk until the consistency of the mixture is smooth and mousse-like.

ASSEMBLY

Using a spoon or a piping bag, spread the filling on half of the biscuits, then top with the remaining biscuits.

note: *if you want to make elongated whoopie pies, like Devil Dogs® (mass-produced American cream biscuits), use the piping bag to form small sausages.*

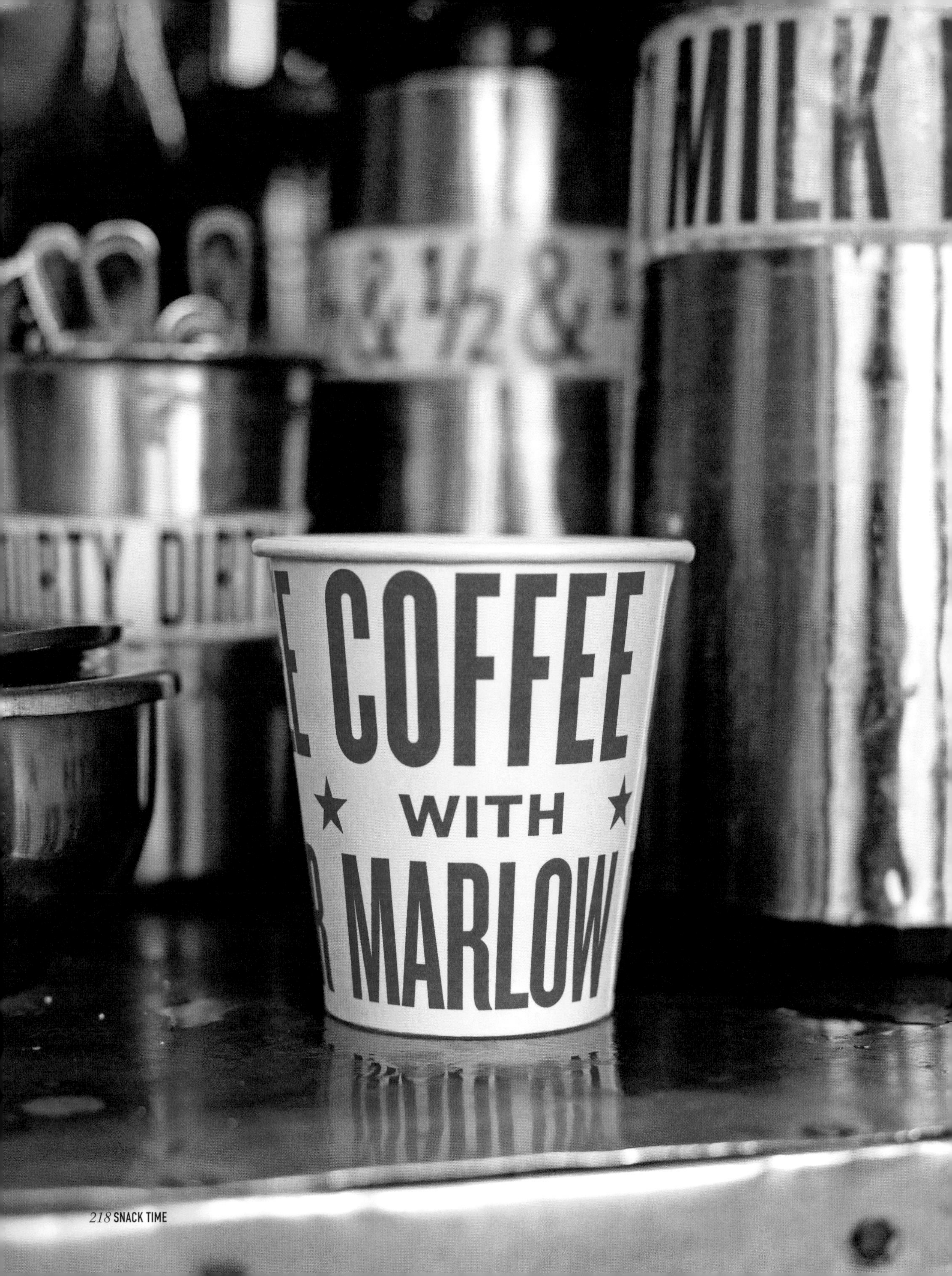
MILK
COFFEE
WITH
MARLOW

BLONDIES

MAKES 16 SQUARES

Preparation time: 20 minutes, plus cooling
Cooking time: 32 minutes

INGREDIENTS FOR WHISKING

150 g (5½ oz) unsalted butter
80 ml (2½ fl oz/⅓ cup) sunflower oil
300 g (10½ oz) raw (demerara) sugar
2 eggs
1 teaspoon natural vanilla extract

DRY INGREDIENTS

300 g (10½ oz /2 cups) plain (all-purpose) flour
2 teaspoons baking powder
½ teaspoon salt
70 g (2½ oz) white chocolate, chopped
(or white chocolate chips)
100 g (3½ oz) pecans, chopped

THE BATTER

Preheat the oven to 180°C (350°F/Gas 4). In a
saucepan, melt the butter over low heat and whisk
vigorously for a few minutes with the oil, sugar, eggs
and vanilla. Remove from the heat. Combine the
dry ingredients, then stir in the butter mixture.

COOKING

Butter and flour a 24 cm (9½ inch) square cake
tin. Pour the batter into the tin. With a wet hand,
flatten and smooth the surface. Bake for about
30 minutes. The cake should be fairly firm to the
touch. Allow to cool, then cut into 16 squares.

BROWNIES

Our answer to the French chocolate fondant cake. A real brownie should be dense, chewy and have a thin, shiny crust on top. You can add nuts if you want. Personally, I prefer to double the amount of chocolate.

MAKES 16 SQUARES

Preparation time: 25 minutes, plus cooling
Cooking time: 40 minutes

INGREDIENTS FOR MELTING

125 g (4½ oz/½ cup) unsalted butter
325 g (11½ oz) dark chocolate
25 g (1 oz) cocoa powder

INGREDIENTS FOR WHISKING

60 ml (2 fl oz/¼ cup) sunflower oil
260 g (9¼ oz) light brown sugar
    (or 250 g/9 oz caster (superfine)
    sugar + 3 teaspoons molasses)
½ teaspoon natural vanilla extract
3 eggs
3 egg yolks

DRY INGREDIENTS

150 g (5½ oz/1 cup) plain
    (all-purpose) flour
½ teaspoon salt
100 g (3½ oz/⅔ cup) dark
    chocolate, chopped

THE BATTER

Preheat the oven to 180°C (350°F/Gas 4). In a saucepan, melt the butter, chocolate and cocoa powder over low heat. In a bowl, whisk the oil, sugar, vanilla, eggs and egg yolks vigorously for a few minutes. Combine the dry ingredients and add them to the whisked mixture, then stir in the melted mixture.

COOKING

Grease and flour a 24 cm (9½ inch) square cake tin. Spread the batter in the tin. With a wet hand, flatten and smooth the surface. Bake for about 35 minutes. The top of the cake will become shiny and start to crack and it should be fairly solid to the touch. Allow to cool and cut into 16 squares.

BROOKLYN CAFÉS

Four & Twenty Blackbirds and Bakeri: these two bakery–cafés are emblems of the 'home-made' ethos and sexy 'low-tech' ambience that has made Brooklyn the hippest neighbourhood in New York.

OPEN DAIL
8 to 7

ICE CREAM $4

Sweet Cream
Buttermilk
Caramel
Mint

12-4

.00
.00
50

50
E 11.50
16.00
2.00
12.50
14.00

PU-ERH   GREEN

BLACK   WHITE   OOLONG   CHAI
         PENNY

CHOCOLATE CHIP COOKIES

I use the same basic recipe to make two versions of this classic cookie: an extra-large one, overloaded with huge and irregular chunks of chocolate and another, mini-sized one, with chocolate chips.

MAKES 18 BIG COOKIES OR 45 MINI COOKIES

Preparation time: 25 minutes, plus cooling
Refrigeration time: 2 hours
Cooking time: 10 minutes

WET INGREDIENTS

250 g (9 oz/1 cup) unsalted
   butter, softened
125 g (4½ oz) caster (superfine) sugar
125 g (4½ oz) light brown sugar (or
   120 g/4¼ oz caster (superfine)
   sugar + 1 teaspoon molasses)
1 teaspoon natural vanilla extract
2 pinches salt
2 eggs

DRY INGREDIENTS

400 g (14 oz/2⅔ cups) plain
   (all-purpose) flour
1 teaspoon baking powder
200 g (7 oz) chocolate, coarsely
   chopped into chunks (or 250 g/9 oz
   chocolate chips for the mini ones)
50 g (1¾ oz) chopped macadamia
   nuts or walnuts (or 50 g/1¾ oz
   extra pieces of chocolate)
1 teaspoon fine sea salt (optional)

THE DOUGH

Beat the butter and sugars in a food processor or by hand until light and creamy. Add the other wet ingredients, beating constantly until smooth.
Combine the dry ingredients — if making mini cookies, substitute the coarsely chopped chocolate with chocolate chips and omit the nuts. Combine the two mixtures until a dough forms. Shape into a ball, cover loosely in plastic wrap and refrigerate for 1 hour.

SHAPING INTO A SAUSAGE (FOR THE BIG ONES)

Take the dough out of the refrigerator, remove the plastic wrap and place the dough on a sheet of baking paper. With the help of the baking paper, shape the dough into a smooth sausage shape about 10 cm (4 inches) in diameter. Wrap the dough in the sheet of baking paper and refrigerate for at least 1 hour.

COOKING

Preheat the oven to 200°C (400°F/Gas 6). Remove the dough sausage from the refrigerator and unwrap from the baking paper. Using a knife or a pastry cutter, cut it into round slices about 1.5 cm (⅝ inch) thick, if making big cookies.
Arrange them on a baking tray lined with baking paper. Bake for about 10 minutes, then allow to cool for at least 10 minutes at room temperature before serving.
If making mini cookies, roll heaped teaspoons of dough into balls and bake for 5–6 minutes. The cookies should still be slightly soft when they come out of the oven. Allow them to cool for at least 10 minutes at room temperature before serving.

note: I discovered the extra touch that sea salt gives from eating a great David's-style chocolate chip cookie at the incredible Bakeri in Williamsburg. Since then, no chocolate chip cookie seems complete to me without this little pinch.

BLACK & WHITE COOKIES

The ultimate New York cookie.

MAKES 9 LARGE COOKIES

Preparation time: 30 minutes, plus cooling
Cooking time: 15 minutes

DOUGH

85 g (3 oz) unsalted butter, softened
100 g (3½ oz) caster (superfine) sugar
2 eggs
115 ml (3¾ oz) buttermilk
½ teaspoon natural vanilla extract
½ teaspoon finely grated lemon zest
250 g (9 oz/1⅔ cups) plain
    (all-purpose) flour
1 teaspoon baking powder
1 pinch salt

WHITE FROSTING

190 g (6¾ oz) icing (confectioners') sugar
1½ tablespoons boiling water

BLACK FROSTING

2 teaspoons unsalted butter
50 ml (1¾ fl oz) thin (pouring) cream
60 g (2¼ oz) dark chocolate, chopped
50 g (1¾ oz) icing (confectioners') sugar
1 teaspoon boiling water

THE DOUGH

Preheat the oven to 180°C (350°F/Gas 4). Using a food processor or a wooden spoon, beat the butter and sugar vigorously until light and creamy. Incorporate the eggs, buttermilk and vanilla, continuing to beat until smooth. Next add the lemon zest and dry ingredients and mix until you have a smooth dough.

COOKING

flRoll 2 tablespoons of dough into balls and place on a baking tray lined with baking paper, leaving 3 cm (1¼ inches) between each. Bake for about 12 minutes until the cookies are lightly browned. Allow them to cool on a wire rack, then return them to the tray.

THE FROSTING

Combine the white frosting ingredients until smooth. Using a brush or spoon, spread this frosting on one half of the flat side of each cookie. For the black frosting, place the butter and cream in a saucepan and bring to the boil over medium heat. Remove from the heat, add the chopped chocolate and let it melt for 1 minute, then add the icing sugar and boiling water. Spread the black frosting on the other half of the cookies. Lay the biscuits on a wire rack to let the icing harden.

tip: if, while standing, the frosting becomes too thick, add a little boiling water to make it easier to spread.

HOME-MADE OREOS®

Here is my recipe for Oreos®, recreating the traditional sandwich cookie at home.

MAKES ABOUT 16 HOME-MADE OREOS®

Preparation time: 25 minutes, plus cooling
Refrigeration time: 2 hours
Cooking time: 15 minutes

WET INGREDIENTS

150 g (5½ oz) unsalted butter, softened
350 g (12 oz) light brown sugar (or
    325 g/11½ oz caster (superfine)
    sugar + 25 g/1 oz molasses)
1 egg, beaten
1 teaspoon natural vanilla extract

DRY INGREDIENTS

165 g (5¾ oz) plain (all-purpose) flour
85 g (3 oz) cocoa powder
2 teaspoons baking powder
2 pinches salt

CREAM FILLING

30 g (1 oz) unsalted butter, softened
30 g (1 oz) coconut oil, at
    room temperature
125 g (4½ oz/1 cup) icing
    (confectioners') sugar

THE DOUGH

Using an electric mixer, beat the butter and sugar vigorously until light and creamy. Combine all the dry ingredients together. Add to the butter–sugar mixture, alternating with the beaten egg and vanilla until smooth. Shape into a ball, cover loosely in plastic wrap and refrigerate for at least 1 hour.

SHAPING THE DOUGH

Take the dough out of the refrigerator, remove the plastic wrap and place the dough on a sheet of baking paper. With the help of the baking paper, shape the dough into a smooth sausage shape about 30 cm (12 inches) long. Wrap the dough in the sheet of baking paper and refrigerate for at least 1 hour.

COOKING

Preheat the oven to 180°C (350°F/Gas 4). Remove the dough sausage from the refrigerator and unwrap it from the baking paper. Using a large knife or a pastry cutter, cut slices about 1 cm (½ inch) thick. Arrange them on two baking trays lined with baking paper, leaving a 2 cm (¾ inch) gap between each. Flatten them slightly with your hands to give them a round and smooth shape, then bake for 15 minutes. Allow to cool at room temperature.

THE CREAM FILLING

Combine all the ingredients with a whisk until smooth and creamy.

ASSEMBLY

Turn over half the batch of biscuits, flat side facing up. Place about 2½ teaspoons of the cream filling in the middle of each and top with the other halves. Press the two cookies together until the cream reaches the edge.

note: for a fluted edge shape, roll out the dough until 1 cm (½ inch) thick and cut out the cookies with a fluted cookie cutter.

ice cream version: you can also use the cookies to make ice cream sandwiches. Put 1 spoonful of ice cream on the flat side of one cookie and top with another cookie, then wrap the sandwich in a double layer of baking paper and foil and store the wrapped ice cream sandwich in the freezer until ready to serve.

MARSHMALLOW

Home-made marshmallow is a real treat. As for other home-made versions of typically mass-produced foods, making your own means you can ensure the quality of the ingredients and customise the recipe to your liking.

SERVES 2

Preparation time: 20 minutes
Cooking time: 20 minutes
Setting time: 5 hours

INGREDIENTS

80 g (2¾ oz) icing
   (confectioners') sugar
4½ teaspoons cornflour (cornstarch)
35 g (1¼ oz) powdered gelatine
240 ml (8 fl oz) water
450 g (1 lb) sugar
175 g (6 oz) glucose or
   sugar cane syrup (see note)
2 egg whites
1 pinch salt
3 teaspoons natural vanilla extract
   (or other flavouring such as
   rose syrup, orange blossom
   water, coffee extract, etc.)

THE TIN

Combine the icing sugar and cornflour. Oil a 25 cm (10 inch) square cake tin and sift about three-quarters of the sugar–cornflour mixture over the oiled surface.

THE MIXTURE

Sprinkle the gelatine over half the water. Place the sugar, glucose syrup and the remaining water in a saucepan over medium heat, stirring until the sugar dissolves. Bring to the boil, then lower the heat to keep on a very gentle simmer for about 15 minutes without stirring. Periodically wipe down the side of the saucepan with a wet pastry brush to clean off any crystallised sugar. Using a food thermometer, monitor the temperature of the mixture — it should reach 120°C (250°F) — then remove from the heat. Add the gelatine to the sugar mixture, mixing with a fork or whisk until it is completely dissolved. Beat the egg whites in an electric mixer with the pinch of salt until stiff peaks form and set aside. Beat the gelatine–sugar syrup with an electric beater until it has more than doubled in size. Incorporate the beaten egg whites, then the vanilla or other flavour, and continue to beat until combined.

SETTING AND SERVING

Pour the mixture into the tin, smooth the top and dust with the rest of the sugar–cornflour mixture. Let it sit for 5 hours at room temperature. Turn out the marshmallow and cut into small cubes. Store covered in the refrigerator.

note: *glucose syrup can be found in specialty stores or supermarkets. Alternatively, you can replace it with sugar cane syrup. But while marshmallows made with sugar cane syrup are great on their own and in s'mores (page 214) or hot chocolate (see page 234), they do not work well for making rice crispy treats (see page 66).*

HOT COCOA & MARSH-MALLOWS

Not to be confused with hot chocolate. The marshmallows on top are really key in this recipe.

SERVES 2

Preparation time: 5 minutes
Cooking time: 5 minutes

INGREDIENTS

1½ tablespoons good quality cocoa
   powder (e.g. Van Houten®)
100 ml (3½ fl oz) sweetened condensed milk
½ teaspoon natural vanilla extract
1 pinch salt
400 ml (14 fl oz) water
marshmallows (as many as you like)

THE HOT COCOA

Combine the cocoa powder with 1½ tablespoons of the sweetened condensed milk. Add the remaining condensed milk, vanilla and salt, then pour everything into a saucepan and heat over medium heat. Gradually add the water, mixing with a spatula. Heat to just below boiling point and serve with cubes of marshmallow.

MUFFINS

See 'banana bread' recipe page 30.

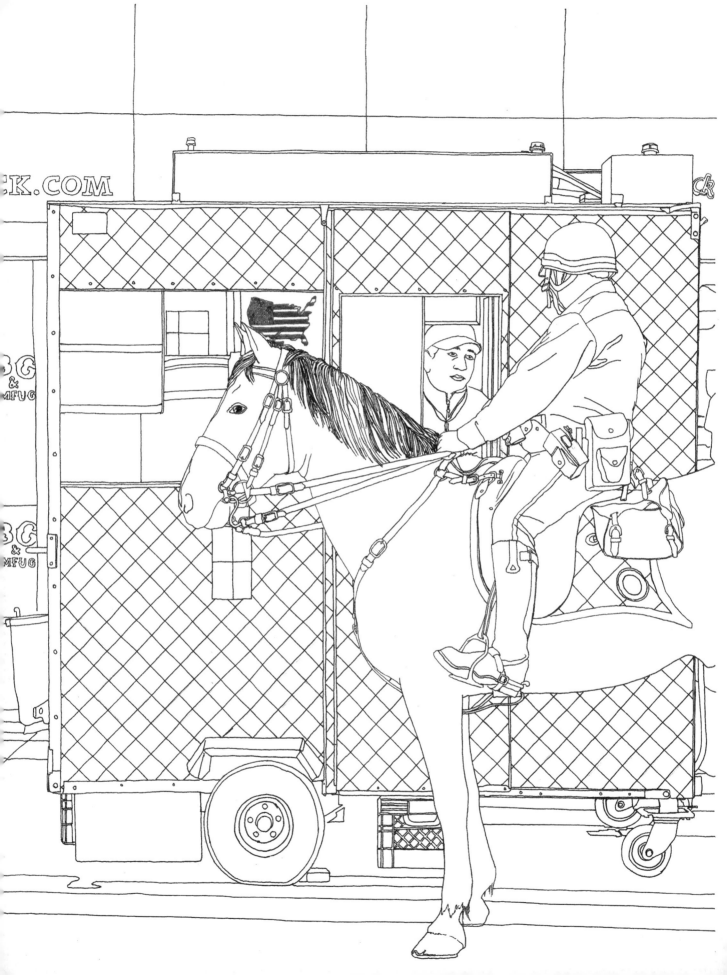

24/24
ANY TIME

EGG IN A HOLE

If you like toast fingers dipped in egg yolk (and who doesn't?), this recipe is for you.

MAKES 1 EGG IN A HOLE

Preparation time: 5 minutes
Cooking time: 2 minutes

INGREDIENTS

1 slice sandwich bread
1 egg
3 teaspoons butter

THE HOLE IN THE BREAD

Using a round cookie cutter or similar — like the cap of a bottle of milk, for example — cut out and remove a circle from the middle of the slice of bread. Place the slice of bread and the circle in a dish.

Break an egg, being careful not to break the yolk, and let most of the white out into the dish with bread, leaving the rest of the white and the yolk in the shell.

Soak the slice of bread and the bread circle in the egg white, turning it over after about 1 minute.

COOKING

Melt the butter in a frying pan over medium heat and, when it starts to sizzle, add the slice of bread. Gently pour the yolk and the rest of the egg white into the hole.

After about 1 minute, slide a thin spatula under the bread and gently turn over onto the other side. Brown for about 1 minute. The aim is to fill and seal the hole with egg without drying out the yolk. Season with salt and pepper.

PICKLES

In a world obsessed with speed, it's good to know that places like The Pickle Guys still exist. They make pickles like in the old days, taking their time, fermenting Kirby cucumbers and other fruits and vegetables for up to three months in refrigerated barrels.

FAST PICKLES

Here are a few of my favourite vinegar pickle recipes.
They are much quicker to make than fermented pickles.

FOR 125 G (4½ OZ) PICKLES
Preparation time: 10 minutes
Cooking time: 5 minutes
Resting time: 24 hours

INGREDIENTS
125 g (4½ oz) vegetables and/or fruit
2 teaspoons pickling spices
   (peppercorns, mustard
   seeds, allspice)
1 bay leaf

BRINE INGREDIENTS
125 ml (4 fl oz/½ cup) water
1½ tablespoons vinegar
1 teaspoon of non-iodised coarse salt
2 teaspoons sugar (optional)

Clean and chop up or slice the vegetables and/or fruit and place them in a heat-resistant container. Add the spices and bay leaf. Combine the water, vinegar, salt and sugar in a saucepan over medium heat. Bring to the boil while stirring. Pour the hot brine into the container. Cover and allow to cool, then refrigerate for 24 hours before serving.

VARIATIONS

spiced pineapple: *rice or cider vinegar, extra 1–2 teaspoons of sugar. Additional ingredient: 2 dried chillies.*

red onion: *red wine vinegar. Additional ingredients: 1 slice cooked beetroot for colour, 3 cloves.*

radish: *rice or cider vinegar.*

Lebanese (short) cucumber: *rice or cider vinegar. Additional ingredient: 1 garlic clove.*

green mango: *rice or cider vinegar. Additional ingredients: 3 cardamom pods, 2 dried chillies.*

carrot: *rice or cider vinegar. Additional ingredients: 3 cardamom pods, 3 cloves.*

SLOW PICKLES

Here is a recipe for traditional salt-water pickles like the ones made by
The Pickle Guys on the Lower East Side of Manhattan and served in most
New York delis and diners. Feel free to adjust the mix of spices to your liking.

FOR 3 OR 4 PICKLES
Preparation time: 15 minutes
Cooking time: 5 minutes
Fermenting time: 5 days (minimum)
  to 4 weeks

BRINE INGREDIENTS
500 ml (17 fl oz/2 cups)
  distilled water + as much
  as necessary for soaking
3 teaspoons coarse non-iodised salt

INGREDIENTS
250 g (9 oz) mini (pickling)
  cucumbers
1 small bunch dill (with its
  flowers if possible)
2 bay leaves
1 garlic clove
3 teaspoons pickling
  spices (see note)

THE BRINE
In a saucepan, bring the distilled water and salt to the boil. When all the salt is dissolved, remove from the heat and cool. This can be done in advance.

THE CUCUMBERS
Wash the cucumbers and remove the blossom ends (as opposed to the stem ends). Unless your cucumbers have just been picked, soak them for 2 hours in distilled water, which will make your finished pickles firmer.

THE JARS
Place the dill, bay leaves, garlic and pickling spices in the bottom of a glass or ceramic container that's just large enough to hold all the cucumbers packed tightly together. After filling with the cucumbers, cover with the cooled pickling brine to 10 cm (4 inches) above the top of the cucumbers. To keep the cucumbers submerged, cover with a small plate weighted with a small cup or a sealed plastic bag filled with brine (you fill the bag with brine in case it leaks). Cover the jar with a clean tea towel (dish towel), a piece of muslin (cheesecloth) or an unsealed lid. Keep in a cool, dark place, outside of the refrigerator.

THE FERMENTATION
Every day or so, remove the scum that forms on the surface and, if necessary, add a little more brine to keep the cucumbers submerged. After 4 or 5 days at room temperature, the cucumbers will be partly fermented; they're what we call 'half sours'. After 3 weeks, they will be completely fermented, or 'full sours'. You then have your pickles. How long you ferment depends on how sour you like your pickles. When they reach that point, you should refrigerate your pickle container, which will drastically slow down the fermentation process.

note: *pickling spices are made up of equal quantities or other combination of peppercorns, mustard seeds, coriander seeds, allspice, etc.*

PUMPKIN MUFFINS

These pumpkin muffins are the taste of Christmas.
The little New York touch is the cream cheese in the middle.

MAKES 10 MUFFINS

Preparation time: 20 minutes
Cooking time: 20 minutes

DRY INGREDIENTS

350 g (12 oz/2⅓ cups) plain
    (all-purpose) flour
3 teaspoons baking powder
150 g (5½ oz) light brown sugar
    (or 140 g/5 oz caster (superfine)
    sugar + 2 teaspoons molasses)
3 teaspoons ground cinnamon
1 teaspoon fine salt
1 teaspoon ground ginger
2 pinches ground nutmeg

WET INGREDIENTS

80 ml (2½ fl oz/⅓ cup) buttermilk
125 ml (4 fl oz/½ cup) sunflower oil
2 eggs
1 teaspoon natural vanilla extract
450 g (1 lb) frozen pumpkin
    purée, thawed
110 g (3¾ oz) plain cream cheese
    (such as Philadelphia®)

THE BATTER

Preheat the oven to 220°C (425°F/Gas 7). Combine all the dry ingredients together. Whisk together the buttermilk, oil, eggs and vanilla. Incorporate the dry ingredients, mixing together quickly. Add the pumpkin purée and stir in without overworking the dough.

COOKING

Lightly grease 10 holes of a muffin tin and fill each halfway with the batter. Add 1 heaped teaspoon of cream cheese in the middle of each and cover with batter to the top of the mould.
Bake the muffins for about 20 minutes until golden and a skewer inserted near the middle comes out clean.

note: see pumpkin pie, page 184, for home-made pumpkin purée. Allow 500 g (1 lb 2 oz) raw pumpkin to make 450 g (1 lb) purée.

POP-TARTS®

This is a home-made version of one of my favourite snacks from when I was a child,
the mass-produced toaster pastries popularised by Kellogg's® under the name Pop-Tarts®.

MAKES 9 SMALL POP-TARTS®
Preparation time: 40 minutes, plus cooling
Refrigeration time: 1 hour
Cooking time: 20 minutes

DOUGH
125 g (4½ oz/½ cup) cold
    unsalted butter, diced
250 g (9 oz/1⅔ cups) plain (all-purpose)
    flour (or 235 g/8½ oz plain (all-
    purpose) flour + 3 teaspoons cocoa
    powder for the chocolate Pop-Tarts®)
½ teaspoon salt
25 g (1 oz) icing (confectioners') sugar
2½ tablespoons cold water
1½ teaspoons lemon juice

CHOCOLATE GANACHE
70 ml (2¼ fl oz) thin (pouring) cream
30 g (1 oz) unsalted butter
120 g (4¼ oz) chocolate, cut into pieces

BLUEBERRY FILLING
110 g (3¾ oz) blueberry jam (page 262)
110 g (3¾ oz) whole blueberries

GLAZE
1 egg yolk
1 teaspoon water

FROSTING
1–2 tablespoons boiling water
225 g (8 oz) icing (confectioners') sugar
85 g (3 oz/¼ cup) raspberry
    jam (page 262)
chocolate sprinkles or coloured
cachous, for sprinkling

THE DOUGH
Cut the butter into the dry ingredients (plain for the jam or with cocoa for the chocolate Pop-Tarts®) using a food processor or knife. Next, incorporate the water and lemon juice by hand until you have a smooth dough. Roll into a ball, wrap in plastic wrap and refrigerate for at least 1 hour.

THE CHOCOLATE GANACHE
In a saucepan, heat the cream and butter over medium heat until they come to the boil. Add the pieces of chocolate. Remove from the heat and let it melt for 1 minute. Stir with a spatula until smooth. The ganache is enough to fill nine Pop-Tarts®.

THE BLUEBERRY FILLING
Combine both the ingredients. The filling is enough to fill nine Pop-Tarts®.

SHAPING THE DOUGH
Preheat the oven to 180°C (350°F/Gas 4). On a floured work surface, roll out the dough into a rectangle about 3 mm (⅛ inch) thick, then cut into 18 small rectangles of the same size and place half of them on a baking tray lined with baking paper.
Flatten the edges of the rectangles slightly with a floured finger, then place 3 teaspoons of filling in the middle of each, being careful to stay away from the edges. Moisten the edges of the rectangles with the filling with your finger and top each one with another rectangle of dough. Avoiding pressing down on the filling in the middle, close the edges by pressing them lightly with a floured finger, and then seal them by pressing more firmly with a fork. Trim the excess dough and, using a sharp knife, make small incisions in the top.

COOKING
Combine the egg yolk and water and brush this mixture over the rectangles. Place in the oven and bake for about 20 minutes until they are well browned. Allow them to cool.

FROSTING
In a bowl, combine the water and sugar until smooth. Using a brush or spoon, spread this frosting on the Pop-Tarts®. Sprinkle over the decorations. For the raspberry frosting, heat the raspberry jam, strain it to remove the seeds and use this coulis instead of the hot water in the plain frosting.

BANANA STICKS

Kids love making and eating these, as do I!

MAKES 8 STICKS

Preparation time: 10 minutes
Cooking time: 5 minutes
Freezing time: 5 hours

INGREDIENTS

4 bananas
150 g (5½ oz/1 cup) dark
    chocolate, chopped
2 teaspoons coconut oil or butter
1½ tablespoons boiling water
    (or more if necessary)
2 teaspoons sugar syrup (page 176)
chopped nuts or coloured
    sprinkles, for decorating

THE STICKS

Cut the bananas in half and insert popsicle sticks into the flat
ends. Individually wrap the half bananas in plastic wrap and
place them in the freezer for at least 5 hours ahead of time.

THE SAUCE

Melt the chocolate with the oil or butter over low heat or in a double
boiler. Mix in the boiling water and sugar syrup. If the chocolate
starts to thicken too much from sitting, add a little hot water.

ASSEMBLY

Holding a frozen banana by the stick, dip it into the chocolate mixture.
Using a pastry brush, brush the chocolate up the sides of the banana and over
the bottom, so that it is completely covered. Lift out the banana and gently
tilt and turn it to allow any excess chocolate to drip off.
Immediately sprinkle over any extra toppings of your choice (chopped
peanuts, for example) before the chocolate sets and place on a baking tray
lined with baking paper.

SERVING

Serve immediately, or return to the freezer. If refreezing, you might want
to let the banana sticks warm up for a couple of minutes out of the freezer
before serving as they can be quite hard when they first come out.

*note: popsicle sticks are available online or in some specialty food stores. You
can also reuse the sticks from store-bought ice creams or replace the popsicle
sticks with something else, like an upside-down disposable teaspoon or a coffee
stirrer. You need to make sure your popsicle sticks are labelled 'food grade'.*

CHOCOLATE PEANUT BUTTER CUPS

*Here's an incredibly easy home-made rendition of the famous
mass-produced Reese's Peanut Butter Cups®.*

MAKES 15 MINI MOUTHFULS

Preparation time: 10 minutes
Cooking time: 5 minutes
Freezing time: 10 minutes

INGREDIENTS

1 tablespoon coconut oil
280 g (10 oz) dark
    chocolate, chopped
150 g (5½ oz) peanut
    butter (page 263)

THE CHOCOLATE

In a saucepan, melt the coconut oil and chocolate together over low heat. Mix with a spatula until smooth.

Stack several small paper cases inside each other: it helps keep the paper pleat intact, otherwise the pressure of the chocolate pushes out the sides and distorts the shape.

Using a ratio of two parts chocolate to one part peanut butter, pour a little of the chocolate–oil mixture into the bottom of a paper case and allow the mixture to set in the refrigerator for a few minutes.

ASSEMBLY

Add a little peanut butter into the middle of each cup, then cover with more of the chocolate–oil mixture. Repeat the process with the other cases and place everything in the freezer for at least 10 minutes.

SERVING

Once the peanut butter cups have frozen solid, you can remove the extra reinforcing layers of paper cases.

Take the cups out of the freezer a minute or so before serving.

MACADAMIA NUT COOKIES

Macadamia nuts and white chocolate — a win-win combination.

MAKES 20 COOKIES

Preparation time: 20 minutes, plus cooling
Refrigeration time: 1 hour
Cooking time: 9 minutes

INGREDIENTS

250 g (9 oz/1 cup) unsalted
   butter, softened
250 g (9 oz) caster (superfine) sugar
350 g (12 oz/2⅓ cups) plain
   (all-purpose) flour
50 g (1¾ oz) baby oat flakes or quick oats
½ teaspoon baking powder
½ teaspoon salt
2 eggs
1 teaspoon natural vanilla extract
125 g (4½ oz) white chocolate, chopped
   (or 125 g/4½ oz white chocolate chips)
125 g (4½ oz) macadamia nuts, chopped

THE DOUGH

Using an electric mixer, beat the butter and sugar vigorously until light and creamy. Mix together the flour, oats, baking powder and salt. In a bowl, whisk the eggs with the vanilla.

Incorporate the dry ingredients into the butter–sugar mixture alternately with the eggs, mixing well after each addition. Finally, add the pieces of white chocolate and the macadamia nuts. Mix again. Shape into a ball, wrap loosely in plastic wrap and refrigerate for at least 1 hour.

CUTTING AND COOKING

Preheat the oven to 200°C (400°F/Gas 6). Divide the dough into 20 balls, place them on two baking trays lined with baking paper, leaving about 3 cm (1¼ inches) between each, and bake them for about 9 minutes. The cookies should still be quite soft when they come out of the oven. Allow them to cool for at least 10 minutes at room temperature before serving.

ICED COFFEE

See recipe page 12.

BLUE
CUP

This recipe is a twist on the traditional acai cup, using blueberries instead of acai berries.

SERVES 4
Preparation time: 5 minutes

INGREDIENTS
300 g (10½ oz) frozen banana
300 g (10½ oz) frozen blueberries
120 g (4¼ oz) avocado
1½ tablespoons maple syrup, honey
    or agave syrup (optional)
60 ml (2 fl oz/¼ cup) water

THE MIX
Blend all the ingredients together in a food processor or blender. If the frozen fruit is too hard, let it thaw for a few minutes before blending. If you don't have a food processor, you could mash everything up with a fork for a chunkier version.
Serve like a frozen yoghurt with toppings such as fresh fruit and granola.

GRANOLA
See recipe page 54.

note: the acai is a Brazilian palm tree whose fruit, acai berries, have a high concentration of blue pigment, a very powerful antioxidant. Unfortunately, acai berries can be a little pricey and difficult to find. I prefer blueberries, which are not only loaded with blue antioxidant pigment but are also easier to source. I happen to think they taste better, too. That said, you can certainly replace the frozen blueberries with frozen acai berries if you find them.

MINI MUFFINS

These little bombshells rework mixtures used in other recipes.

MAKES 30 MINI CHEESECAKES

Preparation time: 25 minutes, plus cooling
Cooking time: 10 minutes
Refrigeration time: 1 hour

INGREDIENTS

1 quantity home-made Oreo®
    dough (page 230)
210 g (7½ oz) plain cream cheese
(25% dairy fat, such as Philadelphia®)
60 g (2¼ oz) caster (superfine) sugar
1 pinch salt
3 teaspoons plain (all-purpose) flour
½ lemon, juice and finely grated zest
200 g (7 oz) sour cream (30% dairy fat)
2 eggs
3 drops natural vanilla extract

MAKES 18 MINI BROWNIES

Preparation time: 25 minutes, plus cooling
Cooking time: 25 minutes

INGREDIENTS

1 quantity brownie dough (page 222)
1 large banana, not too ripe
40 g (1½ oz/¼ cup) peanuts,
    coarsely chopped
1 teaspoon fine sea salt

MINI CHEESECAKES

THE OREO® DOUGH AND CREAM CHEESE

Make the Oreo® dough and cheesecake mixture following
the instructions on pages 230 and 196.

SHAPING AND COOKING

Preheat the oven to 220°C (425°F/Gas 7). Divide the Oreo® dough into 20
small balls. Place 20 thick paper cases, 20 silicone moulds approximately
6 cm (2½ inches) in diameter and 4 cm (1½ inches) high, or two greased and
floured muffin tins on a baking tray. Place a ball of dough in each mould and
spread it over the bottom and side with your fingers, without going to the top
of the mould.
Pour the cream cheese filling on top of the Oreo® dough, filling the moulds to
the top. Bake for about 10 minutes. Allow to cool completely before eating.

MINI BROWNIES

THE BROWNIE DOUGH

Make the brownie dough by following the instructions on page 222.

ASSEMBLY AND COOKING

Preheat the oven to 180°C (350°F/Gas 4).
Butter and flour 12 individual silicon moulds approximately 6 cm
(2½ inches) in diameter and 4 cm (1½ inches) high. Fill the moulds
with the batter to the top. With a wet hand, flatten and smooth the
surface. Cut the banana into slices 5 mm (¼ inch) thick and insert a
round into the batter in the middle of each muffin. Sprinkle the top of
the mini muffins with the crushed peanuts, then the fine sea salt.
Bake for about 20 minutes; the top of the mini muffins becomes solid
to the touch and the inside is melting. Allow to cool for at least
30 minutes before serving.

00:00

EXTRAS

THE BASIC RECIPES

STRAWBERRY JAM

*My colleague, Eugénie, makes her strawberry jam
the old-fashioned way, with no added pectin.*

MAKES 1.25 KG (2 LB 12 OZ)
Preparation time: 20 minutes
Cooking time: 20–25 minutes
Resting time: 12 hours

INGREDIENTS
1 kg (2 lb 4 oz) strawberries
700 g (1 lb 9 oz) granulated sugar
55 ml (1¾ fl oz) lemon juice
vanilla bean, halved lengthways

THE DAY BEFORE
Rinse, dry and hull the strawberries, then cut them in half or quarters
depending on their size. Put them in a bowl, add the remaining
ingredients and combine well. Cover and refrigerate overnight.

PREPARATION
To check whether your jam is ready without a sugar thermometer, you
can use the cold saucer test. In this case, place three small clean saucers
in the freezer at least 30 minutes before you start cooking the jam.

COOKING
Take the macerated strawberries out of the refrigerator and pour into a jam
pan or a large stainless steel saucepan. Bring to the boil over high heat. The
mixture will start to froth up.
Stir the mixture regularly and make sure it doesn't overflow the pan. Carefully
remove any scum that forms on top using a skimmer or a tablespoon. Lower
the heat and continue cooking over medium heat for 20–25 minutes.

THE RIGHT TEMPERATURE
Turn off the heat and place a sugar thermometer in the pan, making sure it
doesn't touch the bottom or the sides. The jam is ready when it reaches 104°C
(220°F). Otherwise, return to the heat until it reaches the right temperature.
Without a sugar thermometer, check the setting point of the jam by dipping
in a tablespoon and lifting it above the pan. If the mixture runs off in a
thin stream, the jam is not ready. However, if it forms drops as it starts to
flow, take out one of the small plates from the freezer and pour 1 teaspoon
of jam onto it: the jam is ready when it sets on contact with the cold plate.
Otherwise, return to the heat for a few minutes before repeating the test.

STORING
Remove the vanilla bean and pour the jam into clean jars. It can be stored
in the refrigerator for 3–4 weeks, or sterilise it for a longer shelf life.

RASPBERRY JAM

*In this raspberry jam of Eugénie's, the scent and
taste of lime goes very well with the raspberries,
but feel free to replace it with lemon.*

MAKES 1.25 KG (2 LB 12 OZ)
Preparation time: 20 minutes
Cooking time: about 15 minutes

INGREDIENTS
1 kg (2 lb 4 oz) fresh raspberries
700 g (1 lb 9 oz) granulated sugar
zest of 1 lime
30 ml (1 fl oz) lime (or lemon) juice

Place the raspberries, sugar, lime zest and juice in a jam pan or a
stainless steel saucepan and heat over high heat. Proceed as for the
strawberry jam. Since raspberries are higher in pectin than strawberries,
the cooking time will be shorter and the jam will set more quickly.

*tip: if you make your raspberry jam this way, you get a jam with a lot of seeds,
which some people may not like. You can put all or some of the raspberries
through a food mill to remove the seeds before you start cooking the jam.*

BLUEBERRY JAM

This is Eugénie's recipe without added pectin.

MAKES 1.25 KG (2 LB 12 OZ)
Preparation time: 20 minutes
Cooking time: about 15 minutes
Resting time: 12 hours

INGREDIENTS
1 kg (2 lb 4 oz) blueberries (wild blueberries if possible)
700 g (1 lb 9 oz) granulated sugar
70 ml (2¼ fl oz) lemon juice (approximately the juice of 1 lemon)
zest of 1 lemon

The day before, pick over the blueberries and pass them very quickly
under cold water to rinse. Place them in a jam pan or a large stainless steel
saucepan and heat to a simmer. Turn off the heat, pour into a large heatproof
bowl and allow to cool. Cover the mixture with plastic wrap, placing the
wrap in contact with the surface of the fruit, and refrigerate overnight.
The next day, return the mixture to the pan, add the sugar and lemon
juice and zest and cook over high heat for about 15 minutes, checking
the mixture regularly with the cold plate test (see 'strawberry jam')
or a sugar thermometer. It should indicate 104°C (220°F). Pour into
clean jars and store in the refrigerator. It can also be sterilised.

APPLE JELLY

MAKES ABOUT 500 ML (17 FL OZ/2 CUPS)
Preparation time: 20 minutes
Cooking time: 55 minutes
Resting time: 8–12 hours

INGREDIENTS
1.25 kg (2 lb 12 oz) granny smith apples (or other cooking apples)
800 ml (28 fl oz) water (for an estimated yield of 800 ml juice)
1½ tablespoons lemon juice
500 g (1 lb 2 oz) sugar
¼ vanilla bean
2 teaspoons butter

THE APPLE JUICE
Roughly chop the apples, including the skin and seeds, and simmer in water for 15–20 minutes. Place the apples in a store-bought jelly bag or a home-made equivalent, then let the juice drip and filter through without pressing for 8–12 hours (ideally overnight). Measure the filtered juice and adjust the amount of lemon juice and sugar proportionally. For example, for 400 ml (14 fl oz) juice, you will need 2 teaspoons lemon juice, 250 g (9 oz) of sugar, and so on.

PREPARATION
To check whether the jam is ready without a sugar thermometer, use the cold saucer test: place three small clean saucers in the freezer at least 30 minutes before you start cooking the jam.

COOKING
Combine the filtered juice with the lemon juice and sugar in a saucepan. Stir constantly over low heat. Once the sugar has dissolved, bring the mixture to a low boil, continuing to stir. Place the sugar thermometer into the mixture at this point, still stirring, until the mixture reaches 104°C (220°F). Turn off the heat and let the jelly stand for 5 minutes, then turn the heat back on to bring the jelly back to 104°C (220°F).

THE RIGHT CONSISTENCY
Instead of or as well as the thermometer method, you can test whether the jelly is ready by spooning 1 teaspoon jelly on one of the plates chilled in advance in the freezer. Start doing this test after about 5 minutes of boiling. The jelly is ready when the mixture sets on contact with the cold plate. If this doesn't happen, repeat the test every 5 minutes until you get the desired result, turning the heat off while you perform the test.

STORING
Mix in the butter and vanilla and transfer the jelly to clean jars. Allow to cool and store in the refrigerator.

GRAPE JELLY

MAKES ABOUT 500 ML (17 FL OZ/2 CUPS)
Preparation time: 20 minutes
Cooking time: 50 minutes
Resting time: 10–15 hours

INGREDIENTS
700 g (1 lb 9 oz) granny smith apples
650 g (1 lb 7 oz) muscat grapes
325 ml water (for an estimated yield of 680 ml/23 fl oz juice)
85 ml (2¾ fl oz) lemon juice
600 g (1 lb 5 oz) sugar

THE JUICE
Roughly chop the apples, including the skin and seeds, and simmer in the boiling water for about 5 minutes. Crush the grapes between your hands or with a potato masher, add them to the apples and water and simmer for another 5 minutes. Cover the saucepan, turn off the heat and let the mixture stand for 2–3 hours.

THE JELLY
Pass the mixture through a medium-hole strainer and allow the mixture to drip through a jelly bag or its home-made equivalent for 8–12 hours, as for the apple jelly. Weigh the filtered juice and adjust the amount of each of the other ingredients accordingly, based on the proportions given above for 680 ml (23 fl oz). Cook and store as described in the recipe for apple jelly.

tip: don't throw away the fruit pulp left in the jelly bag, sieve it to make an excellent apple (or apple and grape) sauce, which you can sweeten or flavour to taste. The flavour of the apple and grape sauce reminds me of lychees.

WHIPPED CREAM

I find whipped cream stabilised with Chantifix® practical, but if you know it will be eaten right away, you can simply leave it out for a more traditional whipped cream.

SERVES 8
Preparation time: 15 minutes

INGREDIENTS
200 ml (7 fl oz) thickened (whipping) cream
2½ tablespoons icing (confectioners') sugar
1 tablespoon Chantifix®, or other cream stabiliser (optional)
1 teaspoon natural vanilla extract

At least 15 minutes before you begin, place the bowl and whisk in the refrigerator along with the cream. Combine the sugar and Chantifix®, if using. Begin whipping the cream with an electric mixer on a low speed. Increase the speed gradually while adding the sugar–Chantifix® mixture through a sifter to avoid lumps. Add the vanilla and continue whipping until the cream is firm.

PEANUT BUTTER

Here's a simple way to make peanut butter at home without a special grinder.

MAKES ABOUT 600 G (1 LB 5 OZ)
Preparation time: 5 minutes

INGREDIENTS
500 g (1 lb 2 oz) peanuts, roasted and salted
40 g (1½ oz) coconut oil
1½ tablespoons peanut oil (for smoothness)
1½ tablespoons acacia or other light honey

Blend all the ingredients together in a food processor until smooth. Add more oil if necessary for the desired smoothness.

KETCHUP

This is my basic recipe. You can experiment with a few twists: replace the rice vinegar with balsamic vinegar, add some chilli with the onions and celery …

MAKES 550 ML (19 FL OZ)
Preparation time: 15 minutes
Cooking time: 23 minutes

STOCK
1 tablespoon finely chopped celery
1 tablespoon finely chopped onion
1 teaspoon olive oil
330 ml (11¼ fl oz/1⅓ cups) water

OTHER INGREDIENTS
140 g (5 oz) tomato paste (concentrated purée)
70 g (2½ oz) caster (superfine) sugar
2 pinches salt
small pinch grated nutmeg
1 tablespoon cornflour (cornstarch)
55 ml (1¾ fl oz) white vinegar

THE STOCK
Sauté the celery and onion in the oil for 3 minutes, then add the water and bring to the boil. Lower the heat and simmer for 10 minutes. Strain, reserving the liquid. You need 330 ml (11¼ fl oz/1⅓ cups) liquid, so add water to make up the volume if needed.

THE KETCHUP
Combine the strained liquid, tomato paste, sugar, salt and nutmeg in a saucepan. Bring to the boil over medium heat, then lower the heat and simmer for 5 minutes, stirring. Blend the cornflour with the vinegar. Pour this mixture into the saucepan and simmer for another 5 minutes, stirring.

SERVING
Allow to cool before serving. Store in the refrigerator in a bottle.

DELI MUSTARD

Here is a simple recipe for a basic deli mustard that would be perfect for hot dogs or knishes.

MAKES ABOUT 500 ML (17 FL OZ/2 CUPS)
Preparation time: 15 minutes
Resting time: 1 day

INGREDIENTS
85 g (3 oz/½ cup) yellow mustard seeds
2 pinches salt
3 teaspoons dried turmeric
2 tablespoons plain (all-purpose) flour
2 tablespoons acacia honey or sugar
300 ml (10½ fl oz) cider vinegar

Grind the mustard seeds into a fine powder in a coffee or spice grinder (or use bought mustard powder). Combine with the salt, turmeric and flour. Mix the honey and vinegar together. Combine with the dry mixture with a fork until smooth. If it seems a little thin, this is normal since the mustard will thicken on standing. Cover and leave out for a day at room temperature for the flavours to mingle a little. Store in the refrigerator.

MAYONNAISE

Make your own mayonnaise. It's easy to do and, more importantly, it will be better than the bought version for a couple of reasons: it will be fresh and you will decide what goes into it. Here's the basic recipe I use.

MAKES 200 G (7 OZ)
Preparation time: 15 minutes

INGREDIENTS
1 egg yolk
1 pinch salt
1 teaspoon sugar
1 teaspoon white vinegar or lemon juice
150 ml (5 fl oz) sunflower or canola oil

VARIATIONS
add 1 or both of the following ingredients:
1 teaspoon dijon mustard
1–3 garlic cloves, crushed

PREPARATION
All the ingredients should be at room temperature to facilitate the emulsion. So if you keep your eggs in the refrigerator, take them out at least 30 minutes ahead of time. If you add garlic, crush it as finely as possible, ideally into a paste using a mortar and pestle.

THE MAYONNAISE
In a deep bowl, whisk everything, except the oil, until combined. Continue whisking while dripping in the oil very slowly. As the mayonnaise starts to thicken, you can add the oil more quickly, but if you add the oil too quickly at the start, the emulsion may not take.

CROUTONS

Croutons are an important element in many soups and salads and, in some cases, such as split pea soup or Caesar salad, I consider them to be an integral part of the recipe.

MAKES ABOUT 450 G (1 LB)
Preparation time: 10 minutes
Cooking time: about 10 minutes

INGREDIENTS
450 g (1 lb) stale bread, cut into equal cubes
100 ml (3½ fl oz) olive oil
45 ml (1½ fl oz) melted butter or your choice of oil
1–2 pinches salt
1 teaspoon dried herbs
½ teaspoon garlic powder (optional)

Preheat the oven to 230°C (450°F/Gas 8). In a bowl, mix together the cubes of stale bread with the other ingredients. Spread them out on a baking tray and bake for about 10 minutes until they are golden brown. You can also cook them in a frying pan. This is a good method if you want to make small batches, say for 3–4 servings of salad. In this case, after mixing the ingredients, fry the croutons over medium heat, tossing and stirring them for 5–10 minutes until they are evenly browned.

tip: *if you use fresh bread, dry it out a little by putting the cubes in a preheated 90°C (200°F/Gas ½) oven for about 10 minutes.*

HOME FRIES

Here is a basic technique to make fries in the oven.

FOR 1 KG (2 LB 4 OZ) VEGETABLES
Preparation time: 10 minutes
Cooking time: 30–45 minutes

INGREDIENTS
1 kg (2 lb 4 oz) root vegetables; allow about 100–200 g (3½–7 oz)
per serve (while pale-skinned potatoes are most common, red-skinned
potatoes, sweet potatoes, parsnips or beetroot are fantastic alternatives)
salt and spices
cooking oil

CUTTING
Preheat the oven to 230°C (450°F/Gas 8). Line a baking tray with baking
paper. Peel and clean the selected root vegetables and cut into small
uniform pieces.

FLAVOURINGS
Place the chopped vegetables in a large bowl and toss in a little salt
and spices (such as ground pepper, herbes de Provence, cumin, etc.)
and combine. Which spices and how much you add is up to you,
but it's better to err on the side of too little, since you can always
add more salt, pepper and condiments to taste at the table.

COOKING
Generously drizzle the vegetables with cooking oil and mix by hand
to coat, adding more oil as needed. Spread the oiled vegetables
out on the baking tray in one layer and bake for 30–45 minutes,
taking the vegetables out of the oven about every 15 minutes to
turn them and ultimately to check whether they're cooked.

COLESLAW

*It's hard to imagine having a burger or any sort of sandwich
for that matter without a side of this classic cabbage salad.*

MAKES 20 SMALL SERVES
Preparation time: 10 minutes
Resting time: 12–24 hours

INGREDIENTS
550 g (1 lb 4 oz) cabbage, core and outer leaves removed
100 g (3½ oz) carrot

DRESSING
40 g (1½ oz) sugar
1½ tablespoons white wine vinegar flavoured with tarragon
60 g (2¼ oz/¼ cup) mayonnaise (page 264)
60 g (2¼ oz) yoghurt
2 pinches salt and ½ pinch pepper

THE CABBAGE AND CARROTS
Shred the cabbage and carrot using a food processor, a knife or a hand-
held shredder or grater. I like it to be shredded as finely as possible.
Whatever method you use, shred the cabbage and carrot to the same size.

THE DRESSING
Combine the dressing ingredients and mix with the cabbage
and carrot. The dressing will at first be quite thick, then it will
thin out as the vegetables release their juices. Let the coleslaw
marinate for 12–24 hours in the refrigerator before serving.

ONION RINGS

Onion rings are just that little bit more special than french fries.

SERVES 2
Preparation time: 10 minutes
Cooking time: 3 minutes per batch

INGREDIENTS
2 large onions, oil for frying

BATTER: WET INGREDIENTS
125 ml (4 fl oz/½ cup) milk, 1 egg

BATTER: DRY INGREDIENTS
70 g (2½ oz) plain (all-purpose) flour
2 tablespoons cornflour (cornstarch)
3 pinches baking powder, 3 pinches sugar
1 pinch salt, 1 pinch paprika

THE BATTER
In a deep-fryer or large saucepan, heat some oil until it reaches 180°C
(350°F). Make the batter by mixing the wet and dry ingredients
together separately. Whisk the two mixtures together until smooth.

THE ONIONS
Peel and cut the onions into slices 1–2 cm (½–¾ inch) thick and separate the
slices into rings.

FRYING
Dip the onion rings into the batter, allowing the excess to drain off, and
fry for about 3 minutes until golden brown, turning them over halfway
through. Start frying by testing the oil with a small ring of onion. If it
cooks too slowly or too quickly, adjust the oil temperature. Make sure
you allow the oil to heat back up for a few minutes between batches.

SERVING
Drain the onion rings on some paper towels. Keep them in an oven preheated
to 100°C (200°F/Gas ½) if not serving immediately. Season with salt.

CHICKEN STOCK

*Transform your chicken carcass into precious stock, a
base ingredient in any number of soups and sauces.*

MAKES ABOUT 2 LITRES (70 FL OZ/8 CUPS)
Preparation time: 10 minutes
Cooking time: 3 hours

INGREDIENTS
250 g (9 oz) cooked chicken carcass (skin and meat removed)
3 litres (100 fl oz) cold water
150 g (5½ oz) onion, 50 g (1¾ oz) carrot, 50 g (1¾ oz) celery
1 bunch parsley, 2 bay leaves
2 teaspoons salt and 1 teaspoon peppercorns

Combine all the ingredients together in a large pot. Bring to the
boil, then lower heat to minimum and cook for at least 3 hours,
uncovered, skimming off any scum that forms on the surface about
every 30 minutes. Cool the stock and strain to remove all solids. There
should be about 2 litres (70 fl oz/8 cups) of stock, which, if not used
immediately, can be stored for several days in the refrigerator or frozen.

note: *a lot of cooks reduce their stock by half or more before freezing. Concentrated
stock can be made into ice cubes and extended with water when used in recipes.*

RECIPE INDEX

INGREDIENT INDEX

ADDRESSES

MANHATTAN

BIG NICK'S BURGER AND PIZZA JOINT
2175 BROADWAY
NEW YORK, NY 10024

The walls of this iconoclastic Greek diner are covered with small handwritten notes and portraits of actors. I recommend the eggs, pancakes, burgers, Greek salad.

BROADWAY RESTAURANT
2664 BROADWAY
NEW YORK, NY 10025

A friendly, no-frills Greek diner, with great eggs, a very good meatloaf and gravy, burgers and other sandwiches. The BLT is made with a religious perfection.

DOUGHNUT PLANT
379 GRAND STREET
NEW YORK, NY 10002

Simply the best doughnuts in New York. The crème brûlée is a marvel.

EISENBERG'S SANDWICH SHOP
174 5TH AVENUE
NEW YORK, NY 10010

This quaint diner is my food-loving brother's favourite when he wants a classic coffee shop meal like a tuna melt sandwich or a matzo ball soup.

HOP SHING RESTAURANT
9 CHATHAM SQUARE
NEW YORK, NY 10038

The authenticity of this Chinese coffee shop is undeniable. Treat yourself to an egg custard pie or a pork bun with a cup of piping-hot filter coffee. You will not be disappointed.

KATZ'S DELICATESSEN
205 EAST HOUSTON STREET
NEW YORK, NY 10002

The oldest delicatessen in New York. They still come up with the goods. I recommend the Katz's Corned Beef. Believe me, it's not for nothing they sell more than 2 tonnes a week.

KOSSAR'S BIALYS
367 GRAND STREET
NEW YORK, NY 10002

This kosher bakery makes the best bialys in New York.

MELVIN'S JUICE BOX
130 WEST HOUSTON STREET
NEW YORK, NY 10012

The warm presence of Melvin and his inspired blends make this my favourite juice bar in Manhattan. I particularly like the PB&J smoothie.

MURRAY'S BAGELS
500 AVENUE OF THE AMERICAS
NEW YORK, NY 10011

Here, the bagels are made the old-fashioned way: hand-rolled and slowly fermented. My favourite: the cinnamon–raisin.

MURRAY'S STURGEON SHOP
2429 BROADWAY
NEW YORK, NY 10024

This tiny Jewish deli is a temple for old continental delicacies: smoked fish, pickled meats, noodle kugle, strudel, rugelach … And you will not find a better smoked salmon bagel anywhere.

PHO PASTEUR RESTAURANT
85 BAXTER STREET
NEW YORK, NY 10013

I've been going to this Vietnamese restaurant (one of the first to open in Chinatown) for years. My pet dishes: caramelised claypot fish and green papaya salad.

RUSS & DAUGHTERS
179 EAST HOUSTON STREET
NEW YORK, NY 10002

This small family deli is an institution for all the dishes from the old continent like smoked salmon, pickled herring and caviar. I expect to take my grandchildren there one day.

SECOND AVENUE DELI
162 EAST 33RD STREET
NEW YORK, NY 10016

They say the pastrami sandwiches from this traditional kosher delicatessen are the best in town. They also make a notable matzo ball soup.

STAGE RESTAURANT
128 2ND AVENUE
NEW YORK, NY 10003

I love this Ukrainian greasy spoon for its Eastern European classics: pierogi, latkes, borscht.

THE PICKLE GUYS
49 ESSEX STREET
NEW YORK, NY 10002

For slowly marinated old-style pickles, there's no place better. Everything from classic Kirby cucumbers to spiced pineapple.

TOM'S RESTAURANT
2880 BROADWAY
NEW YORK, NY 10025

This iconic Greek diner gained its fame from a 1990s television series, but above all it's been the favourite restaurant of Columbia University students for over 70 years.

YONAH SCHIMMEL KNISH BAKERY
137 EAST HOUSTON STREET
NEW YORK, NY 10002

This bakery only does one thing but does it well: knishes.

BROOKLYN

BAKERI
150 WYTHE AVENUE
BROOKLYN, NY 11211

A super-cute café with divine cookies and cakes, all served with excellent coffee. The waitresses in their Norwegian mechanic's overalls also add to the charm of the place.

CAFÉ DE LA ESQUINA
225 WYTHE AVENUE
BROOKLYN, NY 11211

This is the former Wythe Diner, converted into a Mexican restaurant. The atmosphere has stayed intact. This is the perfect place to enjoy tacos, tortilla soup and huevos rancheros, or sip on a spicy lemonade.

EAT CAFÉ
124 MESEROLE AVENUE
BROOKLYN, NY 11222

A locavore restaurant (they only use produce grown within a 250 km/155 mile radius) in the heart of Brooklyn, offering inspired but simple vegetarian cuisine. The multi-grain pancakes topped with caramelised apples are a true delight.

FOUR & TWENTY BLACKBIRDS
439 3RD AVENUE
BROOKLYN, NY 11215

If pies were a religion, this café–bakery in the hip Gowanas Canal neighbourhood in Brooklyn would be its temple. The honey pie is a revelation!

JUNIOR'S
386 FLATBUSH AVE EXT
BROOKLYN, NY 11201

This enormous coffee shop-style restaurant is the benchmark for New York cheesecake. Its reputation is deserved.

MARLOW & DAUGHTERS
95 BROADWAY
BROOKLYN, NY 11211

With its neighbours Marlow & Sons and Diner, this butcher's with old-fashioned charm is part of the hipster back-to-basics movement that has developed in Williamsburg in recent years.

PETER PAN DONUT & PASTRY
727 MANHATTAN AVENUE
BROOKLYN, 11211

This old-style Polish doughnut shop in Greenpoint is the perfect place to enjoy the classics: honey-glazed doughnuts, jam or chocolate doughnuts or the Boston cream.

SMORGASBURG (MARKET)
27 NORTH 6TH STREET
BROOKLYN, NY 11211

On Saturdays, on the bank of the East River opposite Manhattan, this incredible market comes alive, bringing together local artisan producers come to show off their products: craft beer, pickles, snow cones, grilled cheeseburgers and s'mores.

ACKNOWLEDGEMENTS

BEHIND THE SCENES

Rose-Marie Di Domenico – editor
Pauline Labrousse – editor
Eugénie Lopez Ioualalen – head chef
Cécile Mayot – graphic design
Moa Dahlgren – recipe illustrator
Emilie Collet – food preparation

COOKS

Jean-Pierre Ahtuam
Sara Jane Crawford
Dorottya Czegledi
Eugénie Lopez Ioualalen
Gavin Smart
Ngan Tran
Amaury De Veyrac

BIG THANKS

Steven Alan
Sandrine Cooper
Arlette Coron
Gabriel Coron
Élisabeth Darets-Chochod
Paul Feldsher
Jerry Grant
Roslyn Grant
Anne Shapiro-Niel
Emmanuel Le Vallois
Magali Veillon
Ayla Yavin

First published in France in 2012 by Marabout.
This edition published in Australia in 2013 by Murdoch Books.

Murdoch Books Australia
83 Alexander Street
Crows Nest NSW 2065
Phone: +61 (0) 2 8425 0100
Fax: +61 (0) 2 9906 2218
www.murdochbooks.com.au
info@murdochbooks.com.au

Murdoch Books UK
Erico House, 6th Floor
93–99 Upper Richmond Road
Putney, London SW15 2TG
Phone: +44 (0) 20 8785 5995
Fax: +44 (0) 20 8785 5985
www.murdochbooks.co.uk
info@murdochbooks.co.uk

For Corporate Orders & Custom Publishing contact Noel Hammond,
National Business Development Manager Murdoch Books Australia.

Supplies by Élodie Rambaud:
MORA: www.mora.fr

Design © Hachette Livre (Marabout) 2012
Text: © Stephane Reynaud

Publisher: Sue Hines
Translator: Melissa McMahon
Editor: Sophia Oravecz
Food editor: Christine Osmond
Editorial Manager: Livia Caiazzo
Production Manager: Karen Small

Printed by 1010 Printing International Limited, China.

IMPORTANT: Those who might be at risk from the effects of salmonella poisoning (the elderly, pregnant women, young children
and those suffering from immune deficiency diseases) should consult their doctor with any concerns about eating raw eggs.

OVEN GUIDE: You may find cooking times vary depending on the oven you are using. For fan-forced ovens,
as a general rule, set the oven temperature to 20°C (35°F) lower than indicated in the recipe.

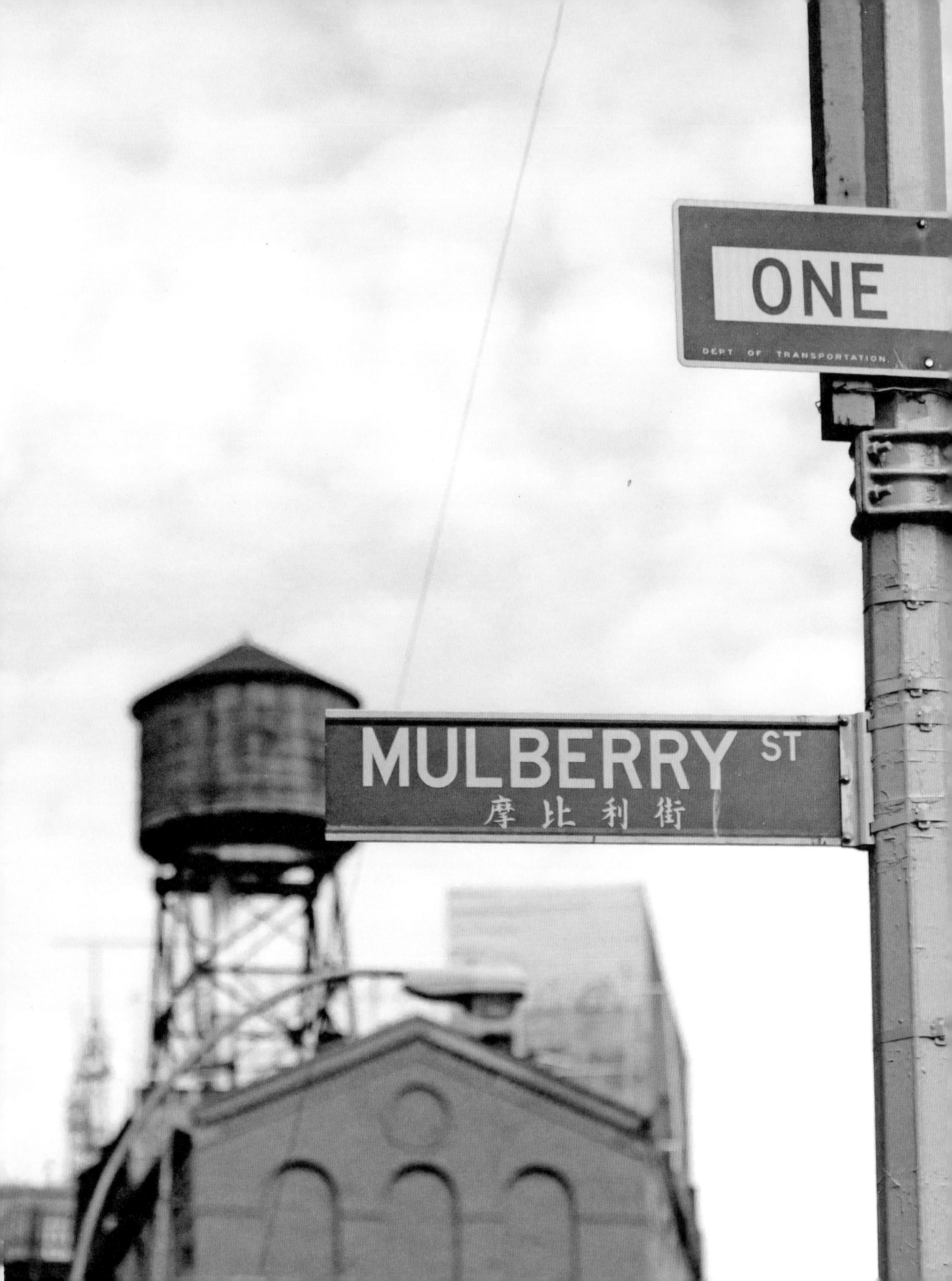
ONE
DEPT OF TRANSPORTATION
MULBERRY ST
摩比利街

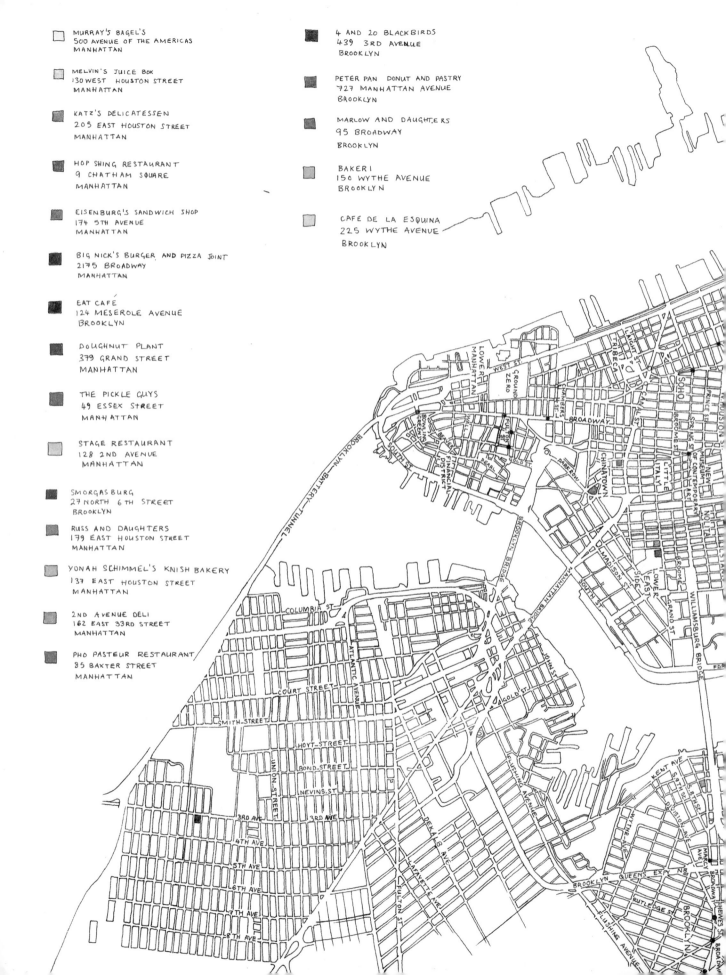

MURRAY'S BAGEL'S
500 AVENUE OF THE AMERICAS
MANHATTAN

MELVIN'S JUICE BOX
130 WEST HOUSTON STREET
MANHATTAN

KATZ'S DELICATESSEN
205 EAST HOUSTON STREET
MANHATTAN

HOP SHING RESTAURANT
9 CHATHAM SQUARE
MANHATTAN

EISENBURG'S SANDWICH SHOP
174 5TH AVENUE
MANHATTAN

BIG NICK'S BURGER AND PIZZA JOINT
2175 BROADWAY
MANHATTAN

EAT CAFÉ
124 MESEROLE AVENUE
BROOKLYN

DOUGHNUT PLANT
379 GRAND STREET
MANHATTAN

THE PICKLE GUYS
49 ESSEX STREET
MANHATTAN

STAGE RESTAURANT
128 2ND AVENUE
MANHATTAN

SMORGASBURG
27 NORTH 6TH STREET
BROOKLYN

RUSS AND DAUGHTERS
179 EAST HOUSTON STREET
MANHATTAN

YONAH SCHIMMEL'S KNISH BAKERY
137 EAST HOUSTON STREET
MANHATTAN

2ND AVENUE DELI
162 EAST 33RD STREET
MANHATTAN

PHO PASTEUR RESTAURANT
85 BAXTER STREET
MANHATTAN

4 AND 20 BLACKBIRDS
439 3RD AVENUE
BROOKLYN

PETER PAN DONUT AND PASTRY
727 MANHATTAN AVENUE
BROOKLYN

MARLOW AND DAUGHTERS
95 BROADWAY
BROOKLYN

BAKERI
150 WYTHE AVENUE
BROOKLYN

CAFE DE LA ESQUINA
225 WYTHE AVENUE
BROOKLYN